Dance Composition

a practical guide for teachers

second edition

Jacqueline M. Smith-Autard

M.A. (University of London)
Diploma of the London College of Dance and Drama
Certificate in Education (University of Nottingham)
A.R.A.D. (Advanced Ballet) L.I.S.T.D. (Cecchetti Ballet, National
Dance, Modern Theatre Dance, Natural Movement, Ballroom and
Latin American)
Principal Lecturer in Dance at Bedford College of Higher Education,
Bedford

A & C Black · London

Second edition 1992
A & C Black (Publishers) Limited
35 Bedford Row, London WC1R 4JH

ISBN 0–7136–3583–5

© 1992 A & C Black (Publishers) Limited

Originally published 1976
by Lepus Books
© 1976 Lepus Books
(An associate company of Henry Kimpton Ltd)

A CIP catalogue record for this book is available
from the British Library.

Cover illustration: Antony Dufort © 1992
Model: Kerry Bell.

Typeset by Florencetype Ltd, Kewstoke, Avon
Printed in Great Britain by Dotesios Ltd

Contents

Preface

In the arts, to compose is to create—to make something which, for each particular artist, has not been in existence before. Artists who attain the highest peaks of perfection in composition; dance—the choreographer, music—the composer, art—the painter or sculptor, drama—the dramatist or playwright, literature—the poet or novelist, are inspired people of imagination and vision. The few who reach these heights of artistry are those with outstanding gifts and skills, and who, through many years of diligent and perceptive study, have mastered their craft so completely that they have no need to analyse the 'rules' when they become inspired to create 'something' which, in its finished form, is unique.

If we are realistic and honest with ourselves, the majority of us know that our talent, in the particular art in which we have chosen to be involved, may have many limitations when compared with those who are truly great. This is not to suggest that we under-estimate ourselves, but that acknowledgement and self-assessment of our own ability is very important as it guards us from becoming pretentious in attempting what is beyond our skill.

The challenge to those who teach through an art is to encourage and guide students towards fulfilling their potential. During the process, the teacher and the taught may derive encouragement and inspiration from each other as well as from those who have been recognised as especially talented.

In this book, dance composition is considered as a craft from the point of view of students and young teachers who are faced with the task of composing dances, and encouraging others to do the same. Many find difficulty in this creative aspect of the art of dance, often through lack of confidence due to insufficient knowledge of the guidelines. But what are the guidelines or 'rules' which become so absorbed and reflected in the works of those who have mastered the craft of their art? This book attempts to answer this question.

Introduction

Dance in Education—
Dancing and Making Dances

Dancing and Making Dances—an Historical Overview.
Dance as Art. The Nature of Composition. The Nature of
Dance Composition. Teaching Dance Composition.

Dancing and Making Dances—an Historical Overview

In the past there has been an over-emphasis on the *act of*
dancing and a lack of attention paid to the *making of dances.*
Both in professional dance and educational dance this would
seem to be true for the young learner-dancer.

In the professional sphere, pupils learn to dance by performing set steps, enchaînements and dances. Few create movement or dances for themselves. Although there are workshops
for young composers in ballet and contemporary dance where
experimentation and exploration take place, there are no
schools that train choreographers as such. Rather, each new
choreographer learns through experience of performing in the
dances of established choreographers. As we will see later in
this book, in education too this strategy is becoming valued,
but it is not considered to be the only way to learn how to
choreograph.

In the sphere of education, the kind of dance which became
the consensus model and a recognised aspect of the school
curriculum in the period 1945–1975 was based on Rudolf
Laban's (1879–1958) approach which is often associated with
the statement in his book 'Modern Educational Dance' (1948):

> In schools, where art education is fostered, it is not artistic
> perfection or the creation and performance of sensational
> dances which is aimed at, but the beneficial effect of the
> creative activity of dancing upon the personality of the
> pupil.

7

This strongly suggests that he considered dancing as an activity valued for what it *feels* like for the dancer. The principal idea behind this statement is that each individual should be allowed the freedom to create *movement* but that the making and performance of *dances* as end products of this creative process is not such a worthwhile aim. So here, too, there is an emphasis on the act of dancing rather than on making dances. As Redfern in 1973 observed:

> . . . it unfortunately often seems to be assumed that because we all have a body and because this is the channel of spontaneous, natural expression, a ready source of dance is at hand, and that one has only to provide some stimulus to switch on and tap this supply.

That this spontaneous natural expression cannot be considered as dance is emphasised in the words of H'Doubler (1957) when she says:

> . . . we do not say that a joyous running and leaping against the wind is art, it is expressive, but it is not expression as art. However, if we take the leaps and runs and various reactions to the feel of the wind and mould them according to the principles of artistic composition, we at once achieve art.

This highlights the difference between dancing and making dances. One enjoys the act of dancing for the pleasure of moving with skilled accuracy, of moving with others, for a release of feeling. But *to create a dance is to create a work of art*, and, according to Redfern (1973) in compliance with H'Doubler (1957), an understanding of dance as an art form begins:

> . . . when concern is not simply with delight in bodily movement but with a formulated whole, a structured 'something' so that the relationship and coherence of the constituent parts becomes of increasing interest and importance.

In the past two decades shifts in dance in education have been rapid and exciting and Redfern's recommendation for an emphasis on creating dances has been fulfilled. We have seen a move away from, or rather a refocussing of, the Laban model, which emphasised the experiential, child centred process of dancing as a means of developing personal qualities, towards a theatre art model with an emphasis on the dance product. The latter, in its professional form, proved too exacting for all but the few who could achieve the heights of technical perfection and polished performance. What we have now is what I like to call a 'midway' model—one that incorporates aspects of both the educational/process/Laban model and the professional/product/theatre model but also pays heed to the distinctive role that dance in education should have in a broad and balanced curriculum.

Dance is a broad concept for there are many forms performed for varied reasons in many differing contexts. To experience a full diet of dance would take up much curriculum time so what we seem to have arrived at, as a consensus approach for dance in education in the 1990s, is a dance as art model which extends across, and draws from, a range of dance contexts—dance in the theatre, dance in the community and dance derived out of specific cultural settings (e.g. South Asian classical dance, social dance, English folk dance).

Dance as Art

The 'midway' model amalgamates some elements of the 'educational' and 'professional' models yet introduces new aspects too. Its distinctiveness lies in the concept of *dance as art education* contributing towards *aesthetic education*. Concentration is centred upon pupils coming to know dance as art through composing, performing and appreciating dances. This three stranded approach has become the central organising principle of dance education today. There is a balance between creating, performing and viewing dances and an overall concern that pupils come to appreciate dances as art works, their own and those produced professionally in theatrical or performance settings.

The first edition of this book published in 1976 provided an important lead in developing and promoting this three stranded dance as art model for education. Since then, others have reiterated justifications for this conceptual basis for dance in education e.g. Adshead (1981), Allcock and Bland (1980), Haynes in Abbs (1987), Lowden (1989). However, there have been no other texts to date which spell out in detail how the three strands may be taught, separately or in integration. This book's concern with dance composition per se leaves the

9

strands of performing and appreciating dances yet to be tackled in a text for teachers. It also pays little attention to an integrated approach* but, in the area of composition alone, it is still an essential text for teachers and students, as it identifies a logical progression in content.

The Nature of Composition

Referring back to Redfern's statement above, composing involves the moulding together of compatible elements which, by their relationship and fusion, form an identifiable 'something'.

The Material Elements

In order to effect this moulding successfully, the composer must be fully aware of the nature of the elements so that he/she may best judge how to select, refine and combine them. Think of the knowledge that necessarily goes into the making of an aircraft, a piece of furniture, a building. Maybe this knowledge is shared among many people, each concerned with a small part of the composition, but considered collectively, the nature of the elements are fully understood before such things can be produced. Without some previous concept or image it takes a great deal of trial and error to fashion anything with elements that are completely foreign.

Methods of Construction

The material elements of the composition need to be experienced and understood and, also, the processes or methods of fashioning or combining these various elements have to be learned and practised. The composer-musician cannot write notes *ad hoc*, they must have relationship to each other in order to create melody. There are rules of construction which help the composer decide how to juxtapose sounds, achieve harmony or discord, change key, vary phrase length and intensity in order to produce mood or expression in the music. The composer also has to adhere to disciplines of rhythm, consider

* 'Dance as Art Education: a new methodology', by Jacqueline M. Smith-Autard is in preparation. This will offer alternative approaches to the teaching of the three strands; dance composition, performance and appreciation. However, this new edition of 'Dance Composition' contains some ideas on how the three strands can be integrated in the context of a resource-based teaching methodology (see Section III).

the effects of tempo and understand how to structure and stylise the piece. The dance composer has also to consider such matters. There are 'rules' or guidelines for construction which need to be part of the composer's awareness when making dances.

From the above discussion it is clear that composition of a successful dance pre-supposes that the composer has knowledge of:

a) the material elements of a dance and
b) methods of construction which give form to a dance, together with
c) an understanding of the style within which the composer is working.

It is to be expected that a pupil who has only just been introduced to the art of making dances will not produce a work of art with the same degree of sophistication as a student having undergone two or three years training.

Through experience and continual practice, the composer gradually acquires knowledge of movement material and methods of constructing the material. The degree of this knowledge affects the resulting level of sophistication in the dance creations.

The Nature of Dance Composition—Dance as Art

From the discussion so far, it is clear that a dance composition should be regarded as a *work of art*. What, then, do we understand by the term *art*?

Mettler (1960) writes:

Art is the shaping of some material to provide aesthetic experience.

For the purposes of this book the term aesthetic will be used in the sense suggested by Reid (1969):

We have an aesthetic situation wherever we apprehend and in some sense enjoy meaning immediately embodied in something; in some way unified and integrated; feeling, hearing, touching, imagining. When we apprehend— perceive, and imagine things and enjoy them for their own sakes—for their form—the forms seem to be meaningful to us, and this is an aesthetic situation. What we thus appre-

11

hend as meaningful is meaningful not in the sense that the perceived forms point to something else, their meaning, as ordinary words or other symbols do: the forms are in themselves delightful and significant—a poem, a picture, a dance, a shell on the sea shore. This then is the aesthetic, which art forms share with objects and movements which are not in themselves art at all. The arts are concerned with the aesthetic but the aesthetic is much wider than the arts.

This would suggest that expression of emotion is not necessarily art. To dance, release emotions and express oneself may well be an aesthetic experience, not only for the performer enjoying the movement for its own sake, but also for the onlooker. The sheer beauty of physical movement is aesthetically appreciated in many fields—athletics, sport, gymnastics, swimming, but this is not art.

A work of art is the expression or embodiment of something formed from diverse but compatible elements as a *whole entity* to be enjoyed aesthetically. It has to be created with the composer's intention to say something, *to communicate* an idea, or emotion. In dance this may be about people, happenings, moods or even about movement itself. The dance composition as an entity can only be a *portrayal* of emotions or ideas. Although sincerity of interpretation is essential in order to be convincing, the dancer does not actually 'feel' what the dance reflects. Rather, the carefully selected movement content is an abstraction from actual feeling or happenings to suggest meanings that are significant to the dance idea.

How the composition is arranged or shaped produces the *form* of the whole. The word *form** is used in all arts to describe the system through which each work of art exists. The idea or emotion which is to be communicated becomes embodied in the form. The form is the aspect which is aesthetically evaluated by the onlooker who does not see every element but gains an impression of the whole. This is particularly relevant to the temporal arts, such as music and dance.

---

* The following definition is appropriate for the word *form* as it is used in this book:

The shape and structure of something as distinguished from its material of which it is composed.

Webster's Dictionary (1966)

This statement is reinforced by Martin (1933):

> Form . . . may, indeed, be defined as the result of unifying diverse elements whereby they achieve collectively an aesthetic vitality which except by this association they would not possess. The whole thus becomes greater than the sum of its parts. The unifying process by which form is attained is known as composition.

Teaching Dance Composition

Teachers in art education, generally, are concerned that pupils eventually move from the experimental 'play' stage to a construction stage in which they make things utilising the various components of the art form. As will be discussed later, pupils may well learn from ready-made dance compositions methods of combining elements to create whole dances. Even when the learner is attempting to replicate an art work emphasis of thought will be directed towards the 'rules' of construction.

In dance, too, we must go beyond the sheer 'activity of dancing' and devote time to the art of making dances. If the pupils are to experience dance as an art form, it is imperative that the dance teacher includes in the work-scheme a consideration of dance composition. Then, in addition to the experiential benefits of dancing, pupils may be guided into the realms of art and develop artistic talents and aesthetic awareness.

This view suggests that a reasonable assumption may be made on the following lines:

a) Knowledge of dance as an art form can only be acquired through experiencing dances, making, performing and viewing them.

b) The basis for success in composition depends upon:
   1) the artistry and intuitive inspiration of the individual,
   2) a wide vocabulary of movement as a means of expression, and
   3) knowledge of how to create the shape and structure of a dance.

For the teacher of dance composition this assumption presents a difficulty. The trend of thought seems to indicate that, apart from knowledge of movement vocabulary and a cursory knowledge of form, dance composition merely requires intuitive artistic insight which is immeasurable and intangible. Although partly an inherited view from the Laban era, there are those who suggest that, because it is so subjective, it is not to be analysed and is, therefore, unteachable. For this reason, perhaps, there is a dearth of literature on the subject. There are many books on the material content of dances but few offering ideas on how this content may be shaped and structured.

The problem of how to achieve form in dance composition with craftsmanship and artistry is the central concern of this book. This is detailed in Section II. A new chapter for this edition has been inserted as *Methods of Construction VI*. This deals with the concept of style and how to stylise a dance composition.

Section I offers a brief discussion of the dance composer's content. It pre-supposes that the reader already has, or will easily acquire from the text, a knowledge of the terminology and concepts offered by Rudolf Laban because, although the philosophy underlying his approach to dance in education is no longer valid, his analysis of movement elements as a basic tool for dance composition is unsurpassed. The concepts identified in his analysis are fundamental because Laban categorised the total range of human movement into easily recognisable and descriptive frames of reference.

Developments in the teaching of dance as an art form clearly demonstrate that the original content of this book outlined above remains relevant as a starting point for teachers and students of dance, whether undertaking professional training, teacher training, B.A. degree courses, G.C.S.E. or 'A' level dance examination courses. It cannot be stressed enough, however, that this book is not in itself a prescribed course for the teaching of dance composition. (No one book can adequately provide all the ingredients necessary for the production of dance art works.) It does, however, disclose the important concepts and principles and offer some means of communicating them to learners. The pupils' imaginative employment of the concepts and principles presented here should be promoted through the teacher's carefully designed programme in which composing, performing and appreciating dances are experienced in a variety of contexts.

To this end, a good deal more material has been produced during the last decade. As well as using books such as this, teachers can enrich dance composing experiences for their pupils from resources such as live performances, videos and films of professional choreography, and/or practical workshops in choreography offered by dance artists resident in schools, colleges or local arts centres. The increasingly available notated scores allow the reconstruction of pre-choreographed dance items. All these are extremely valuable aids in the teaching of dance composition. Such experiences, placed appropriately to supplement the teacher's own input, can effectively motivate, promote and boost pupils' progress in artistic learning.

Use of such a range of resources is exemplified in Section III, a new section for this edition titled—*Resource-based Teaching Learning of Dance Composition*.

Section IV is a new section called—*Standing Back from the Process*. It includes the chapters from the first edition entitled *The Composer's Freedom*, *Evaluations* and *Conclusion*.

Section V consists of some practical assignments derived from and exemplifying the main text. These are designed to deepen understanding in keeping with the contention outlined in this introduction.

Section I

THE MATERIAL
CONTENT:

Movement and Meaning
The Basic Language of Movement. Analysing the Language. Choice of Content. Literal Movement into Dance Content. Exploring a Range of Movement. Movement and Meaning.

The Basic Language of Movement

The word 'language' is used here as an analogy only. It is not meant to suggest that the 'language' of movement can replace or be the same as language in a vocally communicative context. It is common knowledge that communication can take place through movement. How it communicates is the dance composer's area of study. Many verbal expressions describe moods or thoughts in movement terms:

'jumped for joy'	'shrank back in fear'
'rushed into the room'	'bent in pain'
'threw up his hands in horror'	'stamped in anger'
'didn't know which way to turn'	'shook with excitement'

It is this 'natural' movement language which forms the dance composer's vocabulary.

A child's movement is very expressive of his/her feelings. A mother seldom has to ask how he/she feels as she gets to know his/her symptomatic movement patterns. In our culture, it is expected that these are modified as we grow older so that, eventually, it is hard to tell what the typical British 'stiff upper lip' citizen might be feeling. In other cultures, restraint is not so marked, although it is generally accepted that one is not mature if one cannot withhold expression of emotions and moods. Often as much as we try to hide feelings, our involuntary movements and body stance give them away, regardless of what we may be saying vocally. The slumped body stance and slow heavy walk is easily seen to be symptomatic of depression or sadness, the tapping fingers of agitation or anger, the hands clenching and rubbing together of nervousness or fear.

Analysing the Language

The dance composer has this movement language as a basis but requires a means of analysing the content so that he/she may take the symptomatic human behaviour patterns, refine them, add to them, vary them, extract from them, enlarge them, exaggerate parts of them according to the needs in composition. The movement analysis which is most useful and comprehensive is that which Rudolf Laban presents in his books 'Modern Educational Dance' and 'Mastery of Movement'. Although one can refer to it as an analysis, in that it breaks down movement into various components, it does this only in a descriptive way. It is not a scientific breakdown such as is found in the sciences of anatomy, physiology, mechanics, biochemistry. It is a means by which anyone, with knowledge of Laban's principles, can *observe* and *describe* movement in detail.

It is not my intention to describe Laban's analysis in depth for the reader could find this in some of the books listed under further reading on page 158. Table 1 is a simplified version which serves the immediate illustrative purposes.

Choice of Content

Laban's analysis of movement serves the dance composer well because it classifies movement into broad concepts. Each concept suggests a range of movement which may be explored. For example, let us take the concept of 'travel'. This is defined by Laban as a series of transferences of weight from one place to another. The intention is to move from A–B, and the word travel describes this, but it can be done in numerous ways. Each mode of travelling is characterised by the way in which the mover uses action, qualities of movement or dynamics (called effort in the translation of Laban's writings) and space and how the dancer relates the travelling action to an object or person, if this is relevant. In dance, the choice of characterisation depends upon what the mover intends to convey. For instance, to express the joy of meeting the travel may take:

TABLE 1

A SUMMARY OF LABAN'S ANALYSIS OF MOVEMENT

Action of the body	Qualities of movement		
Bend—Stretch—Twist	Time	— sudden	— sustained
Transference of		quick	— slow
weight—stepping			
Travel	Weight	— firm	— light
Turn		relaxed	
Gesture			
Jump—five varieties			
Stillness—balance	Flow	— free	— bound
		(on-	(stop-
		going)	pable)
Body shapes	Combinations of two elements—e.g.		
Symmetrical and	firm and sudden		
asymmetrical use	Combinations of three elements		
Body parts—isolated—	—e.g. light, sustained and		
emphasised	free		

Space Environment	Relationship
Size of movement—	Relating to objects—relating to
size of space	people
Extension in space	Alone in a mass
Levels—low, medium	Duo: copying — mirroring
and high	leading — following
Shape in space—	unison — canon
curved or straight	meeting — parting
Pathways—floor	question and answer
patterns—air patterns	Group work: numerical variation
curved or straight	group shape
Directions in space:	inter-group
the three dimensions	relationship
planes	Spatial relationships—
diagonals	over, under, around
	etc.

the action form of:	leaps, hops, skips, turns, on the balls of the feet, with swinging arm gestures emphasising stretched limbs and body.
the qualities of:	quick, accelerating, light, buoyant, free flowing or continuous.
the spatial form of:	forward in high level, large peripheral movements.

the relationship form of moving towards another dancer.

On the other hand, to express dejection or distress, the travel may take:

the action form of:	a slight run . . . into walk . . . into fall and slide on knees . . . body moving from stretched into curled shape . . . arms gesturing then falling to sides.
the qualities of:	deceleration through the movement from quite quick to very slow, loss of tension from light tension to heavy relaxed feeling, the flow becoming more and more bound/held back.
the spatial form of:	forward direction to low level moving on a straight pathway from centre to forward centre.

Thus the dance composer can use Laban's analysis to help the choice of movement content and depict the intention. He/she can choose the action and colour it with any qualitative, spatial or relationship content he/she likes so that the resulting movement expresses in the composer's own unique way what he/she intends it to say.

There is no *one* way of showing meaning in movement but there are accepted patterns, which define a general area of meaning, and which the composer should employ so that the work can be understood. These originate from the natural symptomatic movement language of humans. Invariably, people of different cultures will interpret what they see in different ways but, even so, there must be some consensus of opinion on such things as mood and idea which the work portrays. For example, if there were strong, striking, fighting, movements between two dancers, agreement will be on 'conflict' rather than 'harmony', or, if the movements were to be slow, gentle, surrounding, supporting, unified in time and complementary in space, it would show 'harmony' rather than 'conflict'.

Literal Movement into Dance

In addition to the major concern for choice of material that clearly identifies meaning, the dance composer has the responsibility of making movement content as original and interesting as possible. To do this Laban's analysis may be used as a frame of reference, and different combinations of action, qualities, space and relationship aspects can be tried. The idea of 'praying' will illustrate this point. Images in the mind of the literal human movement patterns connected with this concept kindles the imagination at the start—hands together, standing with head lowered, a fall on to the knees or even prostration. This range is made more extensive by the composer's analysis and subsequent handling of the movements. For instance, the hands together—head lowered movement can be taken:

action, qualitative and spatial form:

While standing, from an open sideways extension of the arms, trace a peripheral pathway to forward medium, palms leading, slowly bringing the hands together, fingers closing last, with the head back. Then drawing the arms in towards the body centre, allow the chest to contract and curve inwards. To be taken with a sudden impulse at the beginning of the movement into a sustained closing of the hands—with increase of tension from fairly firm to very firm.

OR Move the arms from a symmetric position in front of the head, elbows and wrists bent, successively right then left to diagonally high in front then down to the centre position. This should be done while walking in a forward direction four steps—head moving from low to high—with a firm slow quality throughout. The hands finish close but not touching.

It can be seen from these two examples that by having the basic symptomatic pattern in mind, the composer, through analysis, can identify what it embraces in terms of movement content, its action, its qualitative, its spatial usage and then utilise these aspects in his/her own way enlarging them, high-lighting parts of the actions (e.g. the clasping hands), add actions (e.g. the trunk movement), alter the rhythm and dynamics or the spatial form.

In other words, the composer uses the analysis, first as a means of observing and identifying the nature of the movement as it is in everyday communication, and second, as a means of enriching it into dance content. This should ensure that the movement is both meaningful and interesting. It is difficult to retain a balance between meaning and originality. Care must be taken that the everyday movement origin has not been lost by too much enrichment. Nor should it be presented in the form of cliché which only leads to dull, uninteresting work.

Exploring a Range of Movement

The composer should, therefore, explore and experiment within a wide range, so that he/she becomes fully acquainted with movement and the feeling/meaning connotations. He/she should, at times, set out to explore a full range of movement without using it in composition, for this enriches movement experience and, inevitably, when starting to compose there is a better basis from which to make a choice of content. While exploring the composer will consciously or intuitively experi-ence the expressive properties of the movement, and the feel of it will be stored in the memory for future use. On the other hand, it may be, that while exploring movement for its own sake, an idea is evoked that will make a composition. In this way, movement itself becomes a stimulus for composition as the feeling has acted upon the composer, and then transposed into content. To do this the composer must move from feeling to knowing—knowing what the movement is—analysing it and using its complexity as a starting point for the dance.

If, for instance, the dancer is engaged in exploration of turning as an action, he/she will be led by the teacher's or his/her own knowledge of the analysis, to take the action on both feet, on one foot, on one foot to the other, on different parts of the feet, with hops, jumps, steps, with leg and arm gestures leading into the action across the body or away from the body—producing inward or outward turns—spiralling from low to high and vice versa—taking a wide spread stepping turn—holding the leg high in the air whilst slowly pivoting on the supporting leg—initiating turns with various body parts and many more variations each having its own expressive content. The outward turns may have a feeling of exhilaration, while the hopping, jumping turns also express joy and excitement. An inward closed turn may suggest fear or turning away from something or someone. Turns which increase in speed generate excitement. A slow wandering turn may suggest searching. While the dancer is actually doing the movement, he/she should have some kind of feeling about it. Even if he/she cannot name a mood or emotion that is evoked when it merely feels 'nice', 'good' or 'clever', it carries with it a 'colour' and mode of being. All movements have expressive properties which are employed as a means of communicating ideas about human feelings, events or even about the movements themselves.

Movement and Meaning

It should be clear that movement is a vast communicating language and that varieties of combinations of its elements constitute many thousands of movement 'words'. Also, in the context of a dance, movements have to be understood as meaningful in juxtaposition with others. Very often it is a phrase of actions that portrays a single 'word' meaning, or conversely, one movement can give a whole 'paragraph' of content. To transform a vocabulary of movement into meaningful visual images, the composer is dealing with three intangible elements: movement, time and space. How the meaning can be enhanced by the composer's use of time and space will be discussed later. Meaning in the movement itself is of importance now.

Presentation of literal movement is not dance. The art of mime aims for realistic representation of movement to communicate literal meaning. Dance often uses conventional and mime-based gestures but the composer may choose to manifest the idea in a more symbolic way. This is done by abstracting an essence from the literal movement which then gives a unique flavour through artistic manipulation. This might be analogous to the poet who, rather than make direct statements, uses metaphor and simile to establish images which can have several possible meanings within the poem's context.

23

Although it derives from fundamental human movement, symbolic dance movement imagery can pose several interpretive possibilities. To a certain extent, it depends upon the nature of the audience as to how 'open to interpretation' the composer can make the dance. Some audiences, wishing to be entertained without much effort, require readily recognised movement images, while others tend to enjoy looking more deeply.

The following description of a particular dance may help to explain a little about the range of movement imagery open to a composer, and the scope of interpretation some particular movement images present to an audience.

Solo dance titled 'Confession' . . .
Music—single instrument—slow, smooth, introspective, quiet and harmonic.

1) Movements included:
   a) Closing and crossing movements of arms and legs.
   b) Peripheral arm gestures to cover head.
   c) Opening and extending arms and legs very low to the ground.
   d) Stepping and opening sideways, arms high and to side, wrists flexed palms up, chest high and the head up.
   e) Closing one hand above the other and both hands above head but not touching.
   f) Hands clasped with fully stretched arms in varying directions.
   g) Hands opening and extending with wrists and forearms touching.
   h) Twisting trunk movement with palms of hands near the face.
   i) Forward and backward rocking movements with leg gestures extending just off the ground, arms held close to the body.
   j) Falling to the knees into sideways roll returning to one knee and extending forward.
   k) Turning from open body positions into closed body positions.
   l) Jumps with arms and one leg high in front.
   m) Travel with long low runs and end suddenly to fall.

These are a few examples of the movements in the dance. The description is hardly full enough for the reader to be able to translate it into movement but a range of movement ideas should be apparent and something of the composer's interpretation of the dance idea might have emerged.

2) Interpretations:
   a) Something to do with religious confession. The confessing person feels shame, prays, shows humility, reverence and confidence in receiving forgiveness.
   b) Something to do with confessing a feeling of love. The confessing person feels guilty and afraid yet joyful in the revelation of a hitherto hidden feeling of love.
   c) Something to do with a penitent criminal feeling remorse, shame, self-pity and a dawning of hope in anticipation of freedom.

The composer might have had one of these ideas in mind. The first few movements would suggest an interpretation of the title to each viewer and each would then 'read' the images to fit into the interpretation. If a dance is as 'open' as this, the composer has extended the movement content away from the literal and into the realms of symbolism. The symbols themselves are recognisable in this dance for all the interpretations acknowledge 'confession' but the contexts of the confessions vary. The symbols therefore act as suggestions and finer details of interpretation are left to the viewer's imagination.

Section II

METHODS OF CONSTRUCTION I.

The Beginnings
Stimuli for Dance. Types of Dances. Treatment of Material to make Representational or Symbolic Dance Movement. Improvisation—Selection of Starting Movement for a Dance.

Stimuli for Dance

A stimulus can be defined as something that rouses the mind, or spirits, or incites activity.

Stimuli for dance compositions can be auditory, visual, ideational, tactile or kinesthetic.

Auditory Stimuli

Auditory stimuli include music, the most usual accompaniment for dances. Very often, the dance composer starts with a desire to use a certain piece of music, the nature of which has stimulated a dance idea. There are many kinds of music, and the dance composer must be aware of the nature of the music (emotive, atmospheric, abstract, lyrical, comic, dramatic, architecturally patterned) so that if it is to be used as the accompaniment, it complements rather than conflicts with the idea.

The music not only dictates the kind of dance, but also its mood, its style, its length, phrasing, intensities and overall form. Music, therefore, provides a structured framework for the dance, and the stimulus becomes more than a springboard beginning. If music is used as accompaniment the dance cannot exist without it.

Sometimes, a dance composer may be inspired by a piece of music and, because of its complexity or purity, decide not to use it as accompaniment. In this case, perhaps the quality, or design, in the music could be taken and transposed into dance content. The dance form that emerges need not emulate the form of the piece of music, and, when it is complete, the dance should be able to exist for itself without reference to the stimulus.

Other auditory stimuli include percussion instrument sounds, human voice sounds, words, songs and poems. The mood, character, rhythm and atmosphere of the dance can be structured by these stimuli, but often a dance can exist without the sound accompaniment. For instance, a poem may have been the stimulus, but the dance composer finds he/she cannot interpret all the words into movement, so uses it in a different way. Maybe, it is decided necessary to hear the poem before viewing the dance, or to hear a few lines, which make the essence of it, as punctuation of the movement giving its meaning. On the other hand, once it has stimulated the idea or mood, the dance composer may not need to use the poem at all. The composer may even turn to another source for accompaniment, music perhaps. If, however, the poem is used as accompaniment for the dance, the two must appear to the viewer as inseparable in the manifestation of the idea.

Percussion instrument sounds, human voice sounds, sounds in nature or the environment, often make interesting and dynamic stimuli for dance. Here, the movement interpretation can be purely imitative in quality and duration, or perhaps, the association of ideas related to the sounds could provoke emotional, comic, or dramatic interpretations. Unlike music, there is very little restriction in the way that these stimuli can be used, and the dance composer has to take care that the dance and the sound accompaniment have form which give structural unity.

Visual Stimuli

Visual stimuli can take the form of pictures, sculptures, objects, patterns, shapes, etc. From the visual image, the composer takes the idea behind it, as he/she sees it, or its lines, shape, rhythm, texture, colour, utilitarian purpose, or other imagined associations. A chair, for instance, may be viewed for its lines, its angularity, its purpose in holding the body weight, or it may be seen as a throne, a trap, an object to hide behind or under, an instrument for defending oneself, or as a weapon.

Visual stimuli provide more freedom for the dance composer in that, often, the dance stands alone and unaccompanied by the stimulus. However, the origin of the dance should be made clear if it is to be an interpretation of it.

Kinesthetic Stimuli

It is possible to make a dance about movement itself. Some movement or movement phrase takes on the role of kinesthetic stimulus, and the dance is derived from this basis. The movement, in this case, has no communicative purpose other than the nature of itself. It does not intend to transmit any given idea but it does have a style, mood, dynamic range, pattern or form, and these aspects of the movement, or movement phrase, can be used and developed to form the dance which is an exposition on movement itself.

Tactile Stimuli

Tactile stimuli often produce kinesthetic response which then become the motivation for dances. For example, the smooth feel of a piece of velvet may suggest smoothness as a movement quality which the composer uses as a basis for the dance. Or, the feel and movement of a full skirt may provoke swirling, turning, freely flowing, spreading movements which then become the main impetus for the dance composer.

A tactile stimulus could also become an accompanying object. A very fine piece of material, for instance, could be manipulated by the dancers and form a moving part of the dance, complementing, linking, dividing, enveloping and following the dancers. It is important, however, that the manipulation of the stimulus does not become the overriding part of the dance, the dancers' movement appearing secondary.

Ideational Stimuli

Ideational stimuli are perhaps the most popular for dances. Here the movement is stimulated and formed with intention to convey an idea or unfold a story. If the idea to be communicated is war, immediately the composer's range of choice is limited to movement that will suggest this. Ideas, therefore, have a certain aura of concepts which provide frameworks for the creation of dances. Furthermore, stories or happenings have to be sequentially portrayed in narrative form.

To Conclude

The stimulus forms the basic impulse behind the work and

then goes on to structure it. Some structure the outcome more forcefully than others. Often, several stimuli collectively will influence the work, and perhaps, as in the case of music, the stimulus accompanies the dance.

The dance composer's concern is first, whether or not the stimulus is suitable and how to look at it, and second, how it is to accompany the dance if this is to be the case. This concern may derive from a wish that the dance should portray enough of the stimulus to be clear in intention. Obscurity of purpose will cause it to fail in communication. The stimulus is the basis of the motivation behind the dance. If the composer has deliberately created an interpretation of the inspiration incited by the stimulus, and he/she intends that the dance be understood as such, the stimulus should clearly stand out as an origin, even if it is not present.

This suggests that the dance composer has to decide whether or not successful communication of the idea *depends* upon knowledge of the stimulus as an origin. Perhaps it is not necessary for the audience to know the original stimulus, since the dance outcome, as in the case of a dance inspired by a piece of music which has not been used as accompaniment, may well be able to stand on its own, without reference to the stimulus. Often though, the dance title suggests the original stimulus, enough at least to comprehend the motivation. In any event, whether apparent in the outcome or not, the stimulus dictates the type of dance.

Broad classification of dances is generally quite simple for, like music, or any other art, we accept terms such as Classical, Modern, Ethnic, Jazz, Pop.

Commonly accepted terms are also used when describing types of dance composition more specifically. These include pure, study, abstract, lyrical, dramatic, comic and dance-drama.

A Pure Dance and a Study

We say pure dance when we mean that it has originated from a kinesthetic stimulus and deals exclusively with movement itself.

A study is pure, but a dance can be pure and be more than a study. A study suggests that the composer has concentrated on a limited range of material. For example, a picture may be called a study when it is portraying a bowl of fruit, or a portrait may fit the description. In music, a study is often in one key and perhaps within a certain range of technical skills. The dance study may be confined to one kind of movement, perhaps rise and fall or a scale range of time. A dance which is described as pure, generally has no limitations of movement range. In fact it may have several sections in it, each of which has different movement emphasis.

The movement content in a pure dance may be simpler for the performer than that in a study. The latter often demands more complex movement and aims to show virtuosity and academic understanding of its chosen content.

The ballet 'Etudes' choreographed by Harald Lander provides an example. The total ballet may be classified as a pure dance, yet each small part in isolation can be described as a study. To mention two, there is a study on the 'Plié' section of the barre work, and a study on 'petite batterie', but collectively, the whole ballet gives an overall view of the phases and total rhythm of the ballet class. Because the idea is about a certain style of movement, the ballet is pure in classification. Further examples of pure ballets include George Balanchine's 'Symphony in C' and 'Agon' and Frederick Ashton's 'Symphonic Variations' where the movement itself as interpretation of the music becomes the basis for beautifully formed works of art.

Abstract Dance

Abstract is a confusing term. In the fine art sense, Webster's Dictionary (1966) offers the following definition:

> . . . presenting or possessing schematic or generalised form, frequently suggested by having obscure resemblance to natural appearances through contrived ordering of pictorial or sculptural elements.

Of dance composition, however, the dictionary defines *abstract* as:

> . . . lacking in concrete program or story.

This latter definition is wide and meaningless. If a dance lacks a story it is not necessarily abstract. If it lacks concrete programme it can have no logical development, clear manifestation or communication. In which case it is not a dance. Often, young dance composers think they are 'with it' and very modern if they present a series of unrelated and therefore 'non-programme' movements as an abstract dance. Perhaps it works in the static visual arts for the viewer has time to ponder, look from all angles, and read meaning into it as he/she wishes. The dance audience cannot look and ponder. A temporal art cannot be abstract in this sense of the word, its images must somehow be linked and connected.

If we accept the definition pertaining to fine art, then we see that the dance composer could justifiably portray images which are *abstracted* from the natural and bear resemblance to it. Obscurity, however, should be avoided. There is no time to delve into depths in order to find hidden resemblances to the natural, these should appear easily and very quickly. Maybe several *abstractions* can be put over in the manifestation of one idea, e.g. 'Shape'. The dance is abstract when it is the *result of abstraction*, which is:

> . . . something that comprises or concentrates in itself the essential qualities of a larger thing or several things.
>
> Webster's Dictionary (1966)

Like the 'Shape' dance, a dance entitled 'Magnetism', or a dance entitled 'Time', which portrays a variety of images based upon the phenomenal and human aspects of the concept, could be examples of concentration on 'a larger thing', whereas a dance entitled 'Conformity', which portrays images of following in step pattern, imitating mannerisms, waiting one's turn in a queue, might be an example of concentration upon the essential quality of 'conformity' in several otherwise unrelated things.

Thus, an abstract dance implies that the composer has abstracted some thoughts about one thing or several things, and identifies these through movement images which bear fairly close resemblance to them.

Lyrical Dance

Lyrical dance is a category often used and is quoted in Webster's Dictionary (1966) as:

> . . . a tender dance.   Dance Observer.

In reference to the song as a lyric composition, the dictionary defines it as:

> . . . having a relatively light, pure, melodic quality

31

It is unnecessary to categorise this as a separate type, for it suggests a poetic mood which may well be a dominant characteristic of a pure dance or even an abstract dance. The term 'lyrical', therefore, suggests the quality of a dance.

Dramatic Dance and Dance-drama

Dramatic dance implies that the idea to be communicated is powerful and exciting, dynamic and tense, and probably involves conflict between people or within the individual. The dramatic dance will concentrate upon a happening or mood which does not unfold a story. Dance-drama, on the other hand, has a story to tell and does so by means of several dramatic dance episodes or scenes sequentially arranged. A dance depicting Lady Macbeth's agony of mind would be a dramatic dance, but portrayal of the actual story of Macbeth would be dance-drama.

Because dramatic dance and dance-drama are concerned with emotions and happenings related to people, characterisation is a prominent feature. The composer has carefully to study character and mood in reality, and understand how to dramatise the movement content for dance. This, he/she learns, is done through exaggeration of the action, qualitative or space characteristics, particular development of the rhythmic patterns and emphasis on body shape and stance.

Stress on the qualitative content in movement always tends to give dramatic impact. Also, in a dramatic dance there is nearly always relationship between people, or between an individual and an object, and these relationships are always emotive. However, orientation of the relationship must not remain strictly between dancers and the confines of their space. The composer should take care that the audience also can identify with the dramatic relationships within the dance. Projection of dramatic involvement is a difficult technique in dance composition. The composer must try many ways of putting this across. Perhaps spatial placement, directional alignment and the use of focus are of paramount importance.

Comic Dance

Another category, which must be included, is comic dance. Movement material requires a certain kind of handling if it is to be comic. Essentially original or unusual ways of moving and relating to the environment and other people can be comic.

32

Comic movement might be achieved by making body parts move in peculiarly co-ordinated ways taking them out of their normal space zones. Inverting the stance; performing movements which are usually taken on the vertical plane on a horizontal plane; stressing the use of the face and very small body parts like the fingers or toes, could make comic movement. Perhaps also, the composer should try for the unpredictable in movement. For instance, a very large, grand, sweeping gesture with travel on a circular pathway finished with stillness and just one finger moving up and down!

Very often comic dances are mimetic in nature or have parts which are mimetic. The movement content here can be very representational of real life or, perhaps, have deviations or exaggerations of certain elements which cause comedy.

Mode of Presentation

It is now necessary to discuss *how* the movement content is to be presented by the dance composer.

Supposing a decision has been made on the type of dance to be composed and the accompaniment, if there is any. It is quite probable that the stimulus which prompted the idea brought into the composer's thought images of movement related to his/her own experience, which convey the idea, feeling, mood or happening. For example, 'Sadness' conjures up images of people bent, slow moving, introvert small movements, swaying, hand wringing, head in hands etc. In a dance to depict these human movements exactly as they are in real life, is to utilise the movement in a purely *representational* way. To use these movements, extracting the essence or main characteristics and adding other features in action or dynamic stresses, is to utilise the movement in a *symbolic* way.

To symbolise something suggests that there must be a certain sign or signal which details its origin, and the other aspects of it may be unique and perhaps unreal. For example, a gentle sway in sadness may be taken as a large body movement into side extension followed by a circular upper trunk movement with a turn.

Pure representational presentation is mime and from this extreme there are degrees of representation through symbols to the most 'symbolic' and least representative which is a *nearly* unrecognisable presentation. The word 'nearly' is stressed because if it *is* unrecognisable then it fails. The least representative to reality makes the movement 'open ended' in that there may be quite a number of interpretations as to its meaning. This may be because the signal that the composer chooses to retain is very weak juxtaposed to his/her own unique embellishments. Nevertheless, something within the range of possible representative meaning must be clear to the onlooker.

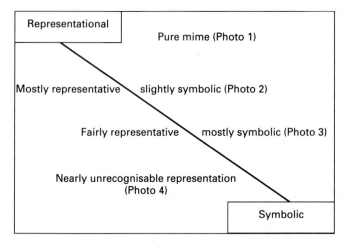

The composer, then, stimulated by his/her own experience of meaning in movement, decides how to present the meaning, representing it as it is in real life, or symbolically portraying it in an original way. Most dances are symbolic presentations of movement, but if they are to be successful the symbols must be identifiable and meaningful to the audience.

Improvisation

The composer has already made some decisions before beginning to move. A decision to use a certain stimulus or several stimuli, has inspired thoughts about the kind of dance to be composed, i.e., comic, abstract, dramatic. In deciding this, the composer has also foreseen the kind of presentation he/she is to use, i.e., symbolic—representational.

Now is the moment to start composing. He/she experiments with movement and tries to realise imagined movement images into real movement expression. This initial exploration is called *Improvisation*.

Improvisation which comes purely from within, a sheer

1.

2.

3.

4.

abandonment in movement to indulge the feeling, is not often the kind of improvisation used by the dance composer. As suggested by H'Doubler (see the quotation in the Introduction) this feeling may well be tapped and recaptured by the composer.

When moving to a piece of music, the improvisation which emerges is less free because the mood and 'colour' of the music suggests the interpretation, and indicates moving in a certain way—governed by the changes in tempo, tone, pitch etc., and its style, form and character. The experimentation with movement is confined to that which is suitable *interpretation* of the music, and this kind of improvisation—although more limited —is commonly used as a starting point.

Improvisation is spontaneous, transient creation—it is not fixed, it is not formed. During improvisation, there are moments when a movement 'feels right' and fits the composer's image. When this occurs, the improvised movement phrase can be recaptured to provide the basic ingredients for the composition. The movement or movement phrase which evolves in this way may be a suitable starting point for the composition process. In evaluating this matter, the composer may use one or more of the following criteria:

1) That the movement has meaning and relevance to the idea for the dance.
2) The movement is interesting and original in action, dynamics and spatial patterning.
3) The movement has potential for development.

This evaluation pre-supposes considerable knowledge of both material and form which is acquired through experience. The apprentice-composer starts from *feeling* not knowing, and may select a movement starting point intuitively. Success is limited, however, if intuition only is relied upon for too long. The reverse can, also, present problems, as knowing without feeling often produces sterile, uninteresting and purely academic dances. Feeling and knowing should always be inter-related. How feeling can consciously be brought into knowing and remain as an artistic stimulus will be discussed later.

The movement starting point is the first piece of composition. It has been selected, evaluated and refined, and is now set as the initial motivating force for the rest of the dance. This movement or movement phrase is called the *Motif*.

The composer continues to employ improvisation in developing, varying and elaborating on the starting motif, and finding new ones for the rest of the composition.

The Beginnings of Composition

Stimulus
|
Decision on type of dance
|
Decision on mode of presentation
Representational or symbolic
|
Improvisation
|
Evaluation of improvisation
|
Selection and refinement
|
Motif

METHODS OF
CONSTRUCTION II.

Motif into Composition

What is a Motif? Development and Variation of a Motif. Repetition as a Constructional Element. Types of Motif.

To Recap

Creativity is a quest for order. When we create we aim for completeness and logical design. Every part of the whole should seem necessary and inevitable.

For the dance to be a meaningful whole it must have recognisable form. A whole is made from a number of components and the dance composer's components include:

1) the dancer's body (or bodies) as an instrument which has volume, shape and action capacities.
2) movement which has physical properties of time, weight, and flow—the interaction of which determines the form and style of the action.
3) the space environment which can be shaped by movement.
4) the relationships that the body can make with other things or people.

Arrangement of Material

How the components are arranged produces the form of the work of art:

> Art expression, like form created by a shifting kaleidoscope, is forever changing, forever new. The myriad of geometric designs that one sees in the kaleidoscope are all made from the same elements, variously shaped pieces of coloured glass but as the relationships of these coloured objects to each other are changed, new forms ensue.
>
> Hayes (1955)

In dances too, the elements of the composer's movement vocabulary are arranged so that they have various relationships to each other. Yet if the dance is successful the patterning or juxtapositioning of movements is *not* the noticeable feature. A gymnastic sequence or skating programme would more favourably fit the analogy with a kaleidoscope, for it is the skilful arrangement of known movement skills that makes successful and aesthetic results in these activities.

Form

A dance aims to communicate an idea and, therefore, there is much more to it than the mere arranging of movements. It has a *form*, an overall shape, system, unity, mould or mode of being. This outer shell, or constructional frame, is the outstanding feature which supports the inner arrangement of its components. Having seen a dance, the viewer does not remember each and every movement or their order. Rather, he/she remembers the impression of the whole, its shape, whether it rounded off as it began, the excitement of the development into the climaxes, the main message it conveyed and how original and interesting was the overall impact.

So the composer has two main tasks. Simultaneously and with artistic awareness he/she should:

1) select movement content, utilising the dancer/s.
2) set the movement into a constructional frame which will give the whole its form.

The Motif Development and Variation

The Motif

There must be *a foundation* for logical development or form. The foundation of a dance is its initial motif. This has emerged during improvisation through the influence of the stimulus, the composer's artistic imagination, and his/her movement interpretation of the two.

Webster's Dictionary (1966) defines the word *Motif* as:

. . . a theme or subject—an element in a composition especially a dominant element.

Langer (1953) says: (author's italics)

The fundamental forms which occur in the decorative arts of all ages and races—for instance the circle, the triangle, the spiral, the parallel—are known as motifs of design. They are not art 'works', not even ornaments, themselves, but they lend themselves to . . . artistic creation. The word motif bespeaks this function: *motifs are organising devices that give the artist's imagination a start, and so 'motivate' the work. They drive it forward and guide its progress.*

39

Some of these basic shapes suggest forms of familiar things. A circle with a marked centre and a design emanating from the centre suggests a flower, and that hint is apt to guide the artist's composition. All at once a new effect springs into being, there is a new creation—a representation the illusion of an object . . . The motif . . . and the feeling the artist has toward it, give the first elements of form to the work; its dimensions and intensity, its scope, and mood.

Preston–Dunlop (1963) states:

A movement motif is a simple movement pattern but it has in it something capable of being developed.

The beginning motif starts to communicate the idea and the next few phrases need to go on saying the same thing as further qualification of the statement. Because dance is transient this restatement is very important. The musician may establish a melody in the opening bars, and then continue repeating the tune developing it and varying it but keeping its characteristics until it has been well established—then, maybe, another melody is introduced which intersperses with the first. The dance composer has also to establish a movement phrase, develop and vary it, so that it becomes known to the viewer, before the dance goes on to say more about the subject.

How is this done? The motif can be as long as a 'verse' or as short as a 'word'. If it is the latter, then, maybe it is necessary to repeat it exactly at the beginning so that it is established clearly. *Repetition of the content, however, is mostly achieved by means of development and variation of the motif/s.*

A Motif

Let us assume that the motif is the simple action of side step and close. This action is taken using the feet for transference of weight, right foot starting. It is danced using a degree of time and force—is hesitant or continuous in flow, moves in a sideways right direction in relation to the body front, which is facing front in relation to the stage space. The rest of the body remains in the normal standing position.

Development and Variation—Using Action Features

The motif could be repeated again exactly, or using the left foot to begin. It could be taken using a different part of the foot to take weight, for instance, on the balls of both feet—on the heels of both—on the ball of the right foot and heel of the left—on the inside edges of the feet—with the weight passing through the balls to the whole foot. There are many ways. It may be that the initiating foot could lead into the side step with the sole of the foot—or side—or ball—or heel—or edge—or top surface. Or, it may be that the closing foot could be used in such a manner, emphasising a leading part, or taking weight in a particular and different way. The action could emphasise the property of stretch, or bend, or twist in the legs, or accompanying body parts. Arm gesture could be added with one or both arms. Leg gesture could be emphasised into the side step, or on the closure, or both. The side and close could be repeated a number of times into a direction of travel, and it could be taken with a turn or change of body front. It could have elevation added to it, into the side step, or the close, or both. It could be taken with a transference of weight onto the knees. Possibly, just the side step could be emphasised leaving out the close, or vice versa. The close step, for instance, could be taken by the right foot in contact with the left leg into standing—or crossing over in front of, or behind the left leg, thereby concentrating on one aspect of the action, extracting it from the rest. The action could be taken with symmetric use of the body, both feet sliding sideways and closing simultaneously with the body evenly placed around its centre. One side of the body could be considerably more emphasised than the other on the side step and perhaps answered by the other side being emphasised on the closing step, giving the whole an asymmetric flavour. Further variation could be achieved by altering the body flow—body parts moving in succession or simultaneously.

Development and Variation—Using Qualitative Features

The qualities or dynamic content of the motif could be developed and varied at the same time as, or apart from, the above action developments. The motif could be repeated faster or slower, with acceleration or deceleration—one part of it could be sudden and the other sustained. Thus the time rhythm of the motif could be varied. The energy stress could be increased or decreased—from strong to gentle qualities. The side step may be taken as a stamp and the close with very little tension or vice versa. Different time and weight combinations could be utilised to give rhythmic patterning. The flow in the motif could be interrupted and held back giving a hesitant

TABLE 2

ACTION

1. Same again – or on other side
2. Use of different body parts
3. Addition of actions – bend, stretch, twist, travel, turn, gesture, stillness, jump, stepping
4. Variation of body flown simultaneous and successive
5. Subtraction of action from motif
6. Symmetric or asymmetric emphasis

SPACE

1. Use of same space pattern
2. Variation of space pattern:
   size
   levels
   extension – near – far
   directions
   pathways – on floor
   in the air
3. Body shape, line in space

QUALITY

1. Same again
2. Speed change
3. Weight variation
4. Time-weight variation
5. Flow variation
6. Contrasting qualities

REPETITION through development and variation by:

RELATIONSHIP

Variation of relationship through changing the juxtapostion of movements within motifs quality, or it could be continuous and ongoing in nature—particularly if a series of side and close steps were taken driving into one direction.

Development and Variation—Using Spatial Features

The composer's use of the space environment could be presented as another means of development. The side and close step could be small, or large, thus defining how much space it takes. It could be taken at different levels, low, medium or high, and in different directions. This latter would be effected by maintaining the sideways direction of the side step in relation to the body front but changing the direction of the body front in relation to the space environment. Whilst this is done, the action of turning must be employed, and a floor pattern will emerge. The shape or pathway that the movement creates in the air may be emphasised as a development feature —for instance, the right leg could gesture into the sideways step with an arc-like action, accompanied by the arms taking a large outward circling movement, and the closing action could be accompanied with an inward circling of the legs and arms, using less space by bending the knees and elbows. The pathways that emerge could be repeated into different directions thus making a spatial pattern.

Development and Variation—Using the Relationship Features

The relationship of the parts of the motif to each other could be altered. The closing step done first, then the side step, thus reversing the order. This is more easily illustrated by taking a longer motif like—travel—jump—turn—still. It could be done in reverse order or in different orders. Parts of it could be extracted, used, and put back into the original juxtaposition.

Repetition as a Constructional Element

The word repetition means *exactly the same thing again*. In the art sense, and in my opinion, the word has wider connotations which could be illustrated as shown overleaf:

Therefore, the notion of repetition as a constructional element implies that the material is manipulated to:

1) Restate or say again exactly—the mover might do identically the same which could be performed with the other side of the body.

43

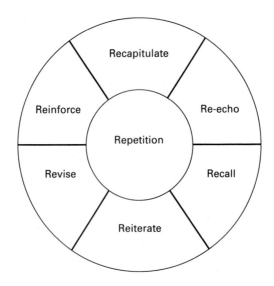

2) Reinforce—making part or the whole of the movement motif more emphasised. This could be done by making the movements larger, or adding more tension or defining the movements by moments of stillness.

3) Re-echo suggests that something of the material which has passed returns into the new content.

4) Recapitulate means that the statements occur again shortening or telescoping the content.

5) Revise—to go over again in some detail, making some parts even clearer.

6) Recall means to bring back into the memory. In the new material the onlooker is reminded of something that has gone before. The content can be dissimilar, but there is an apparent association.

7) Reiterate—stresses the fact of repetition. There may be several continuous repetitions which perhaps die away.

While the composer is using repetition in this expanded sense, a range of developments and variations of the motifs (Table 2, page 42) will inevitably emerge. This should ensure that the content is interesting and yet recognisable as *repeated* material.

Types of Motif

It is impossible to enumerate the types of motif that every dance composer is likely to use. Each dance has its own motifs, and each motif has its own characteristics shared by no other.

It is possible, however, to generalise to a certain extent in description of motifs in terms of length and content emphasis.

Length of Motifs

Some dances use 'positional' motifs. These positions are moved 'into' and 'out of', and act as the landmarks or foundations around which the rest of the dance movement is formed. The motifs, in this instance, are in existence for a short time as momentary positions.

On the other hand, a motif may last for a length of time and could consist of seven or eight movements which create one, two, or even three, movement phrases. It may be that this length of statement is necessary to say one or several things in the dance. It could be presented as a whole, which often happens when the dance is an interpretation of a song or poem. Words in songs or poems are mostly arranged into verse lengths, and the movement can echo this. It is easy for the audience to remember the content because the words in the song or poem become signals for certain parts of the motifs. Very long motifs presented in their entirety without such helpful accompaniment, tend to make it difficult for the onlooker to follow.

Long motifs could be built up piece by piece such as:

```
Movement 1
       "    1          then 2
       "    1            "  2       then 3
       "    1            "  2        "  3       then 4 etc
or Movement 1          then development of 1
       "    2            "        "        "  2
       "    1 and 2 development and variation of both
       "    3 development of 3
       "    1, 2 and 3 development and variation into 4
```

In the final outcome it is only the composer and the dancers who know exactly the length and structure of the motifs which have been used as constructional elements, foundational to the rest of the dance. They need not necessarily be apparent to the onlooker. Unless there is definite association with the stimulus in defining the duration of each motif, their length should be indistinguishable.

Content Emphasis

The nature of the motif may be descriptive in terms of the emphasis it has in content. It is possible to note action, quality or space stresses and follow these aspects as the motivational forces behind the outcome of the dance.

A dance may be space stressed. For instance, the curved shapes and pathways the dancer makes in the space may be the motifs which the audience would view, rather than the action/quality content. In this case the dancer emphasises the shaping of space through projection into the environment and, if successful, the audience will follow these patterns. As a basis for the rest of the dance, the patterns in space then become developed, varied and contrasted into a completed dance form.

The quality content of movement may become the distinguishing feature of the motif. The composer may choose to retain a slow, light and flowing movement quality to establish a quiet feeling and while doing this will use a number of actions. On repeating the quality or developing it, the composer must also concentrate on retaining an identity within the action content. There can be no quality without action. The two cannot really be dissociated, but the slowness, lightness and flowing qualities could be more emphasised than the steps, travels, turns and gestures through which the qualities emerge. The dancer's intention has a great influence on how the audience views the dance. If the dancer concentrates on communication of the quality within the motif, the action content should almost become secondary to it.

An action based motif is perhaps the easiest to handle. Action motifs can be broken down and put together again, since each piece is identifiable as a separate entity e.g. turn, travel, fall, roll, rise, jump. Actions themselves have inherent meanings and emphasis on the action content can make the quality and space aspects less apparent. Nevertheless, the manner in which each action is performed in terms of quality and its spatial usage is all part of its identity.

Movement is an inter-relation of action, quality and space and no one aspect can exist without the other in the motifs, but one or two can be more emphasised. The dance composer could aim for equal emphasis on all three aspects of the movement content in a motif, and make the movement relate to an object or person. The first motif establishes the movement emphasis for that part of the dance. It might be rich in content and become clarified and simplified as the dance progresses or conversely, very simple to start with and become richer and more elaborate during the composition.

For most dances the total range of movement content is available to the composer.

The Dance Design in Time

The Length of Time a Movement Takes

The composer must be concerned that the dance, which exists through time, uses time in a constructive and interesting way. Movement takes time and it is easy to understand that this time can vary in length or duration. The successful composer, therefore, considers the quick, moderate and slow aspects of movement and tries to use them in forming interesting time patterns which are relevant to the idea.

The Length of the Dance

The time aspect is part of the total rhythm of the dance. This is discussed in more detail in Methods of Construction IV. It is enough to mention here that the dance composer should be aware of the total *length* of the dance as vital to the communication of the idea. Dances that are too long lose their impact, and dances that are too short either leave the onlooker surprised and wishing for more, or puzzled—not having had enough to understand the meaning.

The composer should also be aware of the total time picture in relation to the beginning, middle and end of the dance. The beginning may be long, unfolding its content with care, or it may have a vital impact which 'simmers down'. The end may die away gradually into finality or reach a climax after a fairly long middle section. The middle of the dance is too long when the onlooker loses sight of the beginning and does not recognise the end. How the beginning, middle and end share the total time duration of the dance is the composer's decision. There are no set criteria for success in this respect. Each dance demands a different length of time.

47

The Dance Design in Space

The composer must also be concerned that the dance, which exists in space, uses space in a constructive and interesting way.

First, it should be decided how much space to use, relative to the idea and the space available. Second, a decision is made about where the front is, if it is not a stage space, or from which angles the dance will be seen to the best advantage. Then, there are three further considerations:

1) The dancer's shape in space
2) The pathways created on the floor
3) The pathways created in the air

The Dancer's Shape in Space

The dancer's shape in space creates a visual enhancement of the idea behind the movement. The dancer's *feeling* of shape through the kinesthetic sensation of the movement is a very important aspect of presentation of the dance to an audience.

'Feeling' a still shape can cause a sensation of movement and, unless the composer wishes to use absolute stillness for its own sake, every momentary pause or hesitation which retains body shape should create an illusion of movement. This is done by the dancer's feel of stretch, contraction or rotation continuing on into the space or into, or around the body, and by the dancer's focus. The movement in a body shape either lives or dies and the composer should be aware of each body shape as part of the material content which communicates the idea.

The dancer also makes shapes with his/her body as it moves and the onlookers see these shape images transmitted as part of the total expression. Therefore, they need to be clearly defined in movement. Extension and control of the dancer's movement in space are technical necessities for success in this respect.

Aesthetic Quality of Shape in Space

The audience might also enjoy the aesthetic qualities the shapes may embody. If this is to be the case the composer must pay attention to the alignment of the dancer in relation to the front. The body which faces front with the arms and legs on a forward and backward plane loses its shape and line for the audience. It is vital that the perspective and directional implications of placement in relation to the view are considered. (Photos 5, 6, 7, 8 overleaf)

Pathways Created on the Floor and in the Air

The pathways the dance creates on the floor and in the air are living parts of the dance. Curved air and floor pathways create feelings opposed to those which straight air and floor pathways provoke. Most dances have both straight and curved pathways and these can be presented in interesting ways.

The more formal symmetric patterns on the floor may be matched with similar patterns in the air, or vice versa, or, more asymmetric pathways on the floor may be amalgamated with symmetric air pathways or vice versa. To make a symmetric floor or air pattern one would repeat lines or curves on the other side of the body or stage space so that the pattern is evenly distributed. To make an asymmetric floor pattern one would not be concerned to repeat particular lines or curves (see page 51).

Some composers may actually map out a floor pathway for the dance before composing the movement. This might ensure that the dance makes the fullest use of the space and with interesting patterns. On the other hand, in order to guide the emergence of floor and air patterns, some composers would prefer to create the movement by using their natural space patterning inclinations and the spatial characteristics inherent in movement content. Whichever way it is done, the composer should aim to make the spatial design of the dance visually stimulating.

The use of space is further defined by the spatial characteristics of the movements themselves, their level, size, direction and extension.

Motif into Composition

The dance composer, composing for a soloist, is concerned that:

1) the idea is established through the movement content which is organised into motifs, developments and variations.
2) there is enough repetition to confirm the movement images but that repetition is effected in different ways to maintain the onlooker's interest and

49

5. Wrong

6. Right

7. Wrong

8. Right

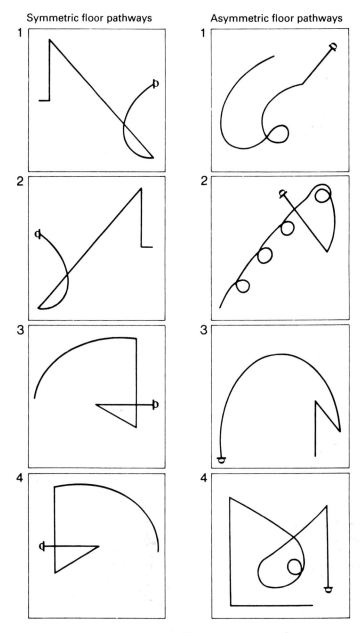

Symmetric floor pathways

Asymmetric floor pathways

51

3) the time and space aspects are interesting and varied and enhance the meaning.

The initial and succeeding motifs, which emerge through the composer's creative response to the stimulus, act as the catalytic agents for the rest of the dance work. If the motifs are 'right' in content and form, the dance stands a chance of being successful.

METHODS OF
CONSTRUCTION III.

Motif into Composition for a Group
The Group as an Expressive Element. Motif, Development and Variation. The Time Aspect. The Space Aspect.

The Group as an Expressive Element
A group dance can be likened to an orchestral portrayal of music. Each of the dancers in the group has a vital part to play in the harmonious, living whole.

Numerical Considerations
The composer should give careful consideration to the number of dancers needed, for every one must contribute to the interpretation of the idea. There are certain expressive connotations which can be related to numbers. For instance, three people always suggest relationship of 2–1. An uneven number of dancers in the group can suggest the isolation of one to induce some kind of conflict, whereas an even number of dancers in the group can unite harmoniously or suggest symmetry and uniformity. Whatever the intention, the composer should be aware of these inherent connotations, though there can be exceptions. A trio, for instance, may well be in harmonious relationship throughout the dance.

Placement and Shape of the Group
The spatial placing and shape of the group has an effect upon the meaning of the movement. A circle facing inwards suggests unity of purpose excluding all focus from the outside world, whereas the same circle facing outwards, without contact, would imply outer interest and non-unity, or, if contact remained, a combination of inner and outer interest. A line, side by side and square on to the front can mean solidarity and unity, whereas a file has sequential connotations.

Consider, also, the expressive nature of a close mass of dancers as opposed to scattered individuals; a large square group opposed to a small circular group; a circle with one dancer in the centre; a wedge or arrowhead shaped group; a group with a single individual apart; a group linked by physical contact; two groups of the same size facing each other. There are endless numerical and placement possibilities in group composition but the meaning of the dance is portrayed by its movement content which either supports or negates these natural numerical, placement and shape expressive implications.

Motif, Development and Variation

Once the composer has established how many dancers to use and how to group and place them, he/she has then to decide how to orchestrate the movement content for the group. A motif may be established by the whole group in unison which then needs repetition and development so that its meaning becomes clear.

The same possibilities of repetition through development and variation of the motifs exist for the group dance as for the solo (see Table 3). Also, an important feature of duo or group composition is the possibility of presenting developments and variations of the movement content at *the same moment in time*. This can be achieved in action, for example, by one person or small group using the other side of the body, or a different body part, or by some members adding other actions to the motif, such as turn and travel. Developments and variations in action, quality, and use of space by the group can be presented as an interesting orchestration of movement content in time and space in the following ways:

The Time Aspect

	UNISON	CANON
a)	Same movements	Same movements
b)	Complementary movements	Complementary movements
c)	Contrasting movements	Contrasting movements
d)	Background and foreground movements	Background and foreground movements

Unison

'In unison' means that the dance movement takes place at the same time in the group and there are four possibilities of presenting unison:

a) Unison: all performing the same movements at the same time. The motif statement is reinforced by sheer multiplicity of numbers. If there are about twelve dancers, the communication is more forceful than if there are only two or three. This

TABLE 3
HOW TO ACHIEVE REPETITION OF MOVEMENT CONTENT
THROUGH DEVELOPMENT AND VARIATION OF MOTIFS
IN DUO OR GROUP COMPOSITION

ACTION
1. Action by doing the same again in unison or canon
2. Action through use of the other side of the body or different body parts
3. Action through addition in action (turn, weight transference, travel, gesture, jump, stillness)
4. Action through extraction of action (part of the movement motif against the whole)
5. Action by changing the body flow, (one group successive another simultaneous)

QUALITY
1. Time–speed constrast within the group
2. Timing–canon–overlapping–sequence
3. Quality variation in Time, or Weight, or Flow, or a combination of these factors within the group

REPETITION through development and variation of

SPACE
1. Design by exact copy or complementing to achieve line repetition, or pathway repetition or shape repetition, or a combination of these
2. Space patterning within the group through variation of:
     size
     level
     direction
     extension
     pathway

RELATIONSHIP
1. Relationship; numerical, placement and group shape variations
2. Juxtapositioning of movement content with the motif or motifs

kind of unison is useful as a start in that the audience has only one movement motif to watch and can identify it quickly and, subsequently, follow the intricacies of its development within the group. Also, it may be that the composer uses all the dancers to create the climax. Unison can be made visually interesting by half the group emphasising one side of the body whilst the other half emphasises the other side.

b) Unison with complementary movements: this implies that movement in the group is occurring at the same time but that the parts of the group are not using identical movement. To complement means to *fill out* or *make more of* and this, in the context of a group dance, may mean that while one part of the group takes the original basic motif, the other part complements it, and, therefore develops it. This can be done by emphasising a different body part, or performing on a different level, in a different direction, with a different amount of extension in space, or by slightly changing all the elements of the motif. By this means, the spectator should be able to appreciate simultaneous repetition of the motif which makes visual re-emphasis of the communication.

c) Unison with contrasting movements: this suggests that all movement takes place at the same time yet the smaller groups within the total group are performing contrasted movement patterns. A few dancers may be taking slow gentle arm gestures while others are doing fast accented foot patterns. This moment in the composition may introduce a new motif in contrast to the original, while the first is still in view. For dramatic purposes, the differences in the movement of the groups may be highlighted. This latter example is quite forceful in presenting opposing material content but it cannot be sustained for long, as it takes a great deal of concentration on the part of the viewer to absorb two simultaneous happenings.

d) Unison with background and foreground: this implies that one part of the group takes on the principal role while the rest of the group moves as a background, subordinate to, and supporting the main part. The dancers in the background might constantly repeat an extract of the motif while those in the foreground present the whole motif, or the background might move very slowly to give the effect of a moving back cloth enhancing the main motif.

Canon

'In canon' means that one part is followed by another in time. The actual amount of time that one part of the group is in front of another can be varied. For instance, one group could start a movement phrase and another group be one moment or several moments behind in time with the same phrase, or maybe, the phrase is only repeated by the second group after it is completed by the first group. The consecutive groups can come in at any time during, or after the initial phrase.

illustrates this point

The sequence in canon can be started by one person and increase in number, or started with a number of people and decrease in number.

Continuous canon gives a sequential effect which may well be a feature of part of a group dance when the dancers take it in turn to do a movement or movement phrase. Single movement canon followed by a phrase canon can add interest to the time aspect of a group dance.

a) Canon with the same movements: the composer may wish to restate the motif by using a small part of the group immediately after the whole group, or he/she may wish to have a short motif repeated in a round-like fashion by several small groups taking turns. Individual dancers within the group could take turns or overlap while performing the same movement content.

b) Canon with complementary movements: this is known as 'question and answer', where one part of the group makes a statement and this is followed by another part of the group making a complementary movement response. The response could overlap, or follow the initial statement.

c) Canon with contrasting movements: here the groups take it in turns or overlap with contrasting movement. The composer may wish to establish two groups in turn and utilise contrasting movement patterns to emphasise their difference.

THE TIME ASPECT

Time ⟶

	Unison	Canon
a)		
b)		
c)		
d)		

∿∿∿ = a movement motif

∧∧∧ = complementary material

▬▬▬ = contrasted material

⎯⎯⎯ = continuous background

- - - - = intermittent background

d) Canon with background and foreground movements: the composer could perhaps establish the background (like a bass introduction to a piece of music) and then bring in the foreground (or melody) during the background movement or immediately after it. The background movement could be used intermittently to punctuate the foreground.

The composer should attempt to use as many of these time aspect variations as are relevant to the idea. By such means, he/she can introduce and repeat the movement content, through development and variation, in unison or canon, in an interesting way within the group. The composer must consider the design of the total length of the dance and the allocation of time for the beginning, middle and end. Methods of Construction II dealt with this aspect. Further discussion on the time design of the overall dance form will continue in Methods of Construction IV.

The Space Aspect

Orchestration of Group Movement in Space

The composer must consider the space aspects to achieve a relatedness of the group throughout the duration of the dance. If the movement were stopped at any moment during the dance, the relationship of the dancers should be as apparent as a visual picture. Dance is a visual art. The composer is producing pictures which range from being fleeting in nature to moments of stillness. There are numerous momentary pictures in a dance and even though the movement may not be stopped, these could be appreciated for their visual design.

The Visual Design of Bodies

The visual design satisfies the onlooker if relationship can be seen. Through perception of the designs of individual members of the group, and groups within the group, the viewer sees this relationship through *exact copy, complementary or contrasting designs*. Exact copy or complementary relationship is made apparent through repetition of line or shape. Contrast can be achieved by some members of the group taking different lines

9. Copying

10. Complementing

11. Complementing

12. Contrasting

13. Complementing and contrasting

14. Copying, complementing and contrasting designs related to the objects and each other.

and shapes. In viewing a group dance, therefore, repetition and/or contrast can be seen to exist in space during each moment of time.

Visual Design as Meaning

The lines and shape each dancer creates with his/her own body in space and through space can be related to those of other dancers, either copying, complementing or contrasting, and this visual picture creates a momentary image which holds meaning for the onlooker (Photos 9–14). A group of dancers emphasising curved body shapes and creating curved pathways in the air and on the floor gives a feeling of rounded, harmonious melodic relationship. This could be contrasted with another group creating straight, angular body shapes, moving in straight lines, which might give a feeling of inter-personal, disciplined and regimented relationship. It is repetition or contrast of the lines and shapes, as well as actions, of the dancers which makes a statement clear. Definition of the group shape in space through such means adds to the statement.

Visual Design as an Aesthetic Quality

Relationship of lines and shapes in space should make the dance a pleasure to view—an aesthetic experience. It is like standing back to view a beautiful cathedral. The 'architectural' design of the bodies, using repetition of line and shape in complementary or opposing directions in relation to the environment, can give a harmonious pictorial effect to the audience. If, on the other hand, discord was the aim the composer would try to eliminate repetition in design at the moment it is to be portrayed.

For the solo dancer or individual members of the group, repetition and contrast of line and shape in the body is also an important aspect. The use of the arms complementing leg shape, the head following the line of the trunk, or the whole body making a shape by virtue of repetition in shape of its multiple parts, or one side of the body contrasting the other, illustrate how the design might add to the aesthetic quality of the dance (see photos 15, 16, 17, overleaf).

Design of the Space

The composer not only has to consider the bodily design of

15.

16.

17.

the dancers and groups in space but also the design or shaping of the space itself.

Shaping the space is done by: (a) creating distance or space between members of the group, and (b) by virtue of movement through space.

Distance or Space Between

The whole of the stage space is available to the dance composer. He/she has to decide how much of it to use and how to use it in relation to the idea.

As soon as two dancers, or two groups, divide, space is created between them and it becomes a living element of the dance expression. If the distance between two groups is too great the composer has destroyed the relevance of the space between, as the audience cannot maintain both moving parts in vision. The nature of the space between is made apparent by the movement content and the dancers' focus—whether it is bonding the two groups, creating a void, or has equal pull from both sides.

As discussed at the beginning of this section, the placing of the dancers or groups in relation to each other suggests meaning. This placing also exposes patterns in space which should be varied as much as possible, within the context of the idea, so that the dance becomes an exciting visual experience for the viewer.

The Pathways Created by Movement

The designs the dance reveals are not only defined by the distance between each dancer and group, but movement itself creates spatial pathways. The design which can be visualised by the audience in retrospect is defined by the movement over the floor and in the air. This is temporal spatial design. The composer should endeavour to make it as interesting as possible and keep it a living and inherently expressive part of the total expression.

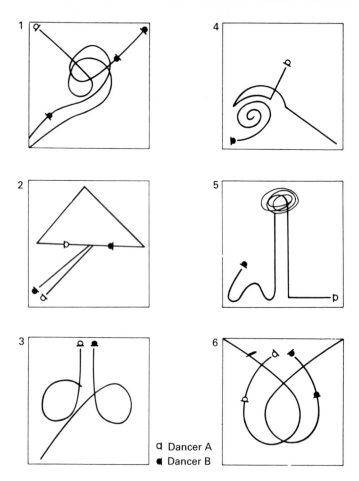

A sequence of spatial patterns created by movement of two dancers over the floor

ꓒ Dancer A
◖ Dancer B

To Conclude

The dance composer who is working for a group, or within a group, is concerned that:

1) the idea is established through the movement content which is organised into motifs, developments and variations.
2) there is enough repetition both in the present and as part of the time construct. Repetition in the present is seen in the design of each dancer or group in relation to the others and in the simultaneous developments and variations of motifs within the group. Repetition as part of the time construct is seen through repetition of design or group shape in canon and development and variation of motifs in canon.
3) the orchestration of the group in time and space is interesting and varied and enhances the meaning behind the dance and makes it a rich visual experience for the onlooker.

METHODS OF
CONSTRUCTION IV.

The Dance Form
Motif into Phrases, Sections. Types of Form.

Design in Time

The composer seeking form for the dance should consider that he/she is creating a design in time. This could be called a time picture. Like any picture it is built up from parts. Once the overall meaning is apparent, the parts fit into a shape or *form* which supports them. An analogy to architectural design illustrates this point. Each part of a building must blend into the whole. Even though each can be viewed for itself, it is its relationship with the other parts that give it meaning. The gables, archways and turrets, for instance, fit into the overall structure defining its shape and style.

Architectural design is static—we can see it all at once. On viewing a dance, however, we can only perceive one piece at a time and we have to put the pieces together in our minds to form a picture of the whole. Since the experience lasts through time, it demands that the dance composer makes the dance pieces by dividing time.

The motif is used as a structural basis for the form. There will nearly always be more than one motif, and different outcomes from each motif must somehow merge into the whole mass with clarity and significance. The motifs themselves create time pictures by the movement which lasts an amount of time, has changing intensities and accents, pauses and stops.

Movements and Movement Phrases

The beginning motif has in it a 'word', or a few 'words', giving a clue to the meaning of the whole. The motif may last in time just as a single 'word' or as a long 'sentence'. If it is the latter it is considered a movement phrase, which has a shape and logical time picture.

The phrase may start by dynamic, shouting, climactic movement and tail off to a calmer ending, or vice versa, or, build up to an explosive middle part and calming down end. So the phrase is structured into a *rhythmic pattern*. The next phrase could take on a different rhythm using the same movement

66

again, but developed, in a different order. Each consecutive phrase makes clearer the idea by re-emphasising the same point, exposing a different view of the same thing, unfolding more content to support the point or even contrasting it by an opposite to give emphasis to the meaning.

Sections

Phrases are usually bound together into sections. A section in a dance may be described as a collection of phrases which are connected – possibly derived from the first phrase which forms the motif, or made up from the inter-relationship of two phrase motifs. A new section would appear with the introduction of new material.

Rhythm and Form

Movements, phrases and sections making patterns in time are some aspects of the rhythm of the dance. From this, it follows that every movement has rhythm. The energy which starts the movement, keeps it going and stops it, is given rhythmic shape by application and release of force within its duration of time. The force, or accents, punctuate and divide the time. Going back to the previous examples—a strong quick accent may begin the movement and then it may become slower and less strong to finish in a dying away manner,

or the build up could come in the middle of the movement or phrase,

or the end of the movement or phrase may become the most forceful giving a climax to the whole.

Inter-relation of the time and weight factors provide the dance composer with a vast range of rhythmic possibilities.

The time picture created in the dance may be symmetrical with the force or accent appearing at regular intervals. This is known as a metric arrangement where the time between the accents is measured out evenly. It can be matched with musical measurements in time e.g., $\frac{4}{4}$. Each metre of time lasts for the same duration, but rhythmic variation can occur within each (see diagrams opposite).

An asymmetric measurement of time is sometimes called breath rhythm. Here the measurements between accents are not even. The movement phrase has its own rhythm, the commas and full stops coming in arbitrarily with the natural feeling of the phrase.

Organisation of the Form

The organisation of time and force in relation to each movement (whether it is quick, slow, accelerates, decelerates; has strong or light accents at the beginning, in the middle, or at the end of it; or increases or diminishes in force throughout its duration) and the organisation of these movements into phrases and sections determines the nature of the dance form. The style and quality of each movement motif will perhaps determine contrasting sections or sections which grow one from the other. The composer then has to consider the *ordering of the sections into a form or design in time*.

There are many ways of organising the form, and each dance should have its own unique structure but, because music is often used as accompaniment and dictates the overall form, musical forms have long been recognised frameworks into which dances are classified whether with musical accompaniment or not. These include Binary, Ternary, Rondo, Theme and Variations and Fugue arrangements.

Binary Form

Binary form is commonly used in dance composition. The first Section A is contrasted by a new Section B, but both have a common thread which binds one to the other like brother and sister. Each section may have contrasting elements, but there

Some Divisions of Time in $\frac{4}{4}$

1 whole note Semibreve	= 4 beats
¹/₂ notes Minims	= 2 beats each
¹/₄ notes Crotchets	= 1 beat each
¹/₈ notes Quavers	= ¹/₂ beat each
¹/₁₂ notes Triple quavers	= ¹/₃ beats each
³/₁₆ and ¹/₁₆ notes Dotted quaver-semi-quaver	= ³/₄ and ¹/₄ beat each
¹/₁₆ notes Semi-quavers	= ¹/₄ beat each
¹/₃₂ notes Demi-semi-quavers	= ¹/₈ beat each

Various rhythmic arrangements within the time duration of 4 beats

must be something similar in nature too. Perhaps the movement in Section A is predominantly slow and gentle and that in
Section B, fast and strong, but the action patterns or spatial
shape may be the same or similar. On the other hand, maybe it
is only the dance idea that binds them together, each section
taking a different aspect of the idea, but in this case too, there
must be something else that relates them—perhaps the style of
movement.

Ternary Form

Ternary form A.B.A. is a conventional and satisfying form
because going back to the beginning 'rounds it off'. Somehow
this produces a comfortable and pleasant 'knew what was going
to happen' feeling in the onlooker. The return to Section A can
be achieved by exact repetition of the initial section, or by
reversing, highlighting parts, changing a few elements and
changing the order of elements. They must, however, be very
closely akin whilst the B. Section forms the contrast.

Rondo Form

Rondo form A.B.A.C.A.D.A. and so on, provides the composer with a verse and chorus framework which gives room for
variation in the verses and development in the choruses.
Variation can produce something new each time, but it must
still have enough of the original to be considered a related part
to the whole. Development can recall the origin in many ways
without changing the essence. Again, this is a conventional and
satisfying form to watch providing it is interesting enough. The
onlooker can quickly identify the chorus movement and enjoy
its repetition. It is like enjoying a song chorus. Through feeling
a kinesthetic sympathy with the dancer it becomes a 'joining-in'
process.

Theme and Variations

Theme and variations is a freer, more asymmetric and exciting form. The theme provides the basis for the variations. This
is often called a sequential form in that the initial statement is
followed by a number of developments or variations. The
initial statement is not made again, and each variation becomes
a basis for the next variation. Therefore the dance can finish
with movement which is very different from that of the beginning. It is like watching a film when you do not know how it is

to end. The composer has a freedom but must pay attention to connectedness throughout. Even if the initial movement phrase is not repeated, something of its nature should linger in the mind of the onlooker so that, on reflection, he/she appreciates the range of variations which have emerged.

Canon or Fugue

Canon or Fugue is a composition in which one or two themes, or motifs, are repeated or initiated by successive dancers. These would then be developed in continuous interweaving of parts into a well-defined single structure. Dance studies in groups can usefully employ this form.

Narrative Form

Narrative form is not derived from musical form. The word narrative suggests that there is to be a gradual unfolding of a *story* or *idea*. The movement content is sequentially arranged into sections, A.B.C.D.E.F.G. etc., and each section is a further exposure of the idea or story.

If the dance conveys a series of images on one idea, the composer has the problem of linking each section so that each naturally flows into the next in a logical sequence. If the dance tells a story (dance-drama) the composer should make the parts adhere very closely. The sections in it should not always be apparent to the onlooker, although the composer may well find it useful to consider it section by section to ensure that there is richness, contrast, and variation in each part of the whole.

To Conclude

The above forms appear cut and dried and easy to distinguish one from the other. However, many dances are not true to the conventional forms and may be an amalgamation. For instance, a dance may start with an A.B.A. form shape, and then go on with C.D. and back again to A; or may follow rondo form, but each new section could follow on narrative lines whilst the A. section remains a chorus.

There are numerous possibilities open to the composer in the arrangement of the overall form. The essential thing to remember is that each part of the dance must have relevance to the whole.

It might be useful to think of a dance having outer and inner rhythmic forms. The inner rhythmic form consists of the time/force shape each movement, movement phrase and section creates, while the outer rhythmic form consists of the shape brought about by the juxtaposition of each section in the dance.

In the illustration below it can be seen that each movement has a rhythm, each of the phrases has a different rhythmic structure, and that the overall shape has an A.B.A. rhythm — the B. section forming a contrast to both As.

A

B

A

METHODS OF
CONSTRUCTION V.

Elements of Construction

Several elements of construction have already emerged in the discussion on the construction of a dance. It may be useful to convey these in a list so that the reader can select each element and evaluate its constructional purpose in any given dance:

1) The Motif/s (Foundation/s of Construction)
2) Repetition
3) Variation and Contrasts
4) Climax or Highlights
5) Proportion and Balance
6) Transition
7) Logical Development
8) Unity

Each of these elements could be discussed in relation to many forms of art. Each element is related to, and complements, the others. All serve unity which is the overall aim in any art. To achieve unity the other seven elements of construction must be employed.

The Motif/s or Foundation/s of Construction

In Methods of Construction II and III, we have discussed the function of the motifs in composition in some depth. It remains to say that these dominant elements of the composition only emerge as dominant in the light of all the other constructional devices used.

Without repetition, the motifs would be forgotten.

Without variation and contrast, repetition of the motifs would be dull if presented ad lib in their original form.

A dance lacking climax or highlights would seem to have motifs which have no content worth highlighting.

Without careful proportioning and balancing of the whole work each of the motifs could become almost eliminated or even too dominant.

Without transitions the motifs would be isolated movement statements. Transitions between each movement within the motif and between the motifs are important in defining the phrase and section shaping of the dance.

Without logical development from motif to motif the theme of the dance would be blurred.

The motifs contain the main ingredients which provide the unifying threads for the whole work. These include the style, qualitative colour, light and shade, line and shape in space, and types of action which motivate the rest of the work.

Repetition

From the preceding text, repetition must be recognised as a main device in dance composition. It should be clear that repetition in a dance exists in the form of development and variation of the movement material which is established within each motif. Also that, in the context of dance as an art form, the word repetition has wider interpretations than its normal usage.

Variation and Contrasts

These elements of construction differ but complement each other. Variation demands that the content, which has already been established in the dance, is *used again* in a different way. Contrast demands the introduction of *new* material either within the original motif during a repetition, or as a variation of the motif. The new material can be another motif of course.

A successful dance should feature both these elements. Variation gives an interesting logical development to the whole providing the necessary means for repetitions of the theme, so that the audience can view it in different ways with growing understanding. Contrasts provide the exciting changes which colour the dance and stand out as points of reference in relation to the total material content. Contrasts can be effected in many ways, and often—though not always—provide the climaxes or highlights in a dance.

To make a contrast, the composer should consider a change in content but this should not be done for the sake of contrast alone. It must also be relevant to the idea behind the dance. In quality content, for instance, the slow section could be followed by a fast section, or the predominantly slow section could have a fast movement to break the continuity of slowness. In spatial content predominantly small low level movements could be contrasted by a large high level movement. In action a phrase containing stepping, gesturing and travelling could be contrasted by jumping; a phrase using one side of the

74

body could be contrasted by one movement of the other side; predominantly symmetrical body action could be followed by a sudden change to asymmetric use of the body.

Contrast is not only achieved through sudden changes in content. It is possible to build gradually towards a contrast. Movement might accelerate from slow into quick, show little tension and increase in strength to show a great deal of tension, start low and gradually grow to high level and so on. Contrast emerges as contrast if the predominant material content is interrupted or punctuated by fresh or opposing movements. It would seem that the opposite, or near opposite, in content is a requisite feature of contrast.

Climax or Highlights

Many people think that a dance should have only one climax, the rest of the material content supporting it. In fact, a dance can have many highlights which may or may not be real climaxes too. In retrospect, the moments which are remembered are highlights of the dance and remain of special significance to each particular viewer. In a work of art, no two people view in the same way, and no two people would necessarily agree on the highlight moments in a dance. If, however, these moments come to fruition in one big climax and this is the intention of the composer, then everyone should see and agree that this is *the* climax. It depends upon the nature of the dance and the idea whether there is one climax or several climaxes or whether these are merely highlights without the especially noticeable features of a 'super' climax. These latter features may emerge with a sudden attack, or build up slowly to an explosive moment. For instance, if the dance has been earth-bound and gestural, a sudden series of leaps accompanied by the trunk twisting, bending and stretching will make a contrast which is also a climax. On the other hand, a climax could be seen as the ultimate development of a motif. In all events, if it is a real climax it should stand out very prominently. Highlights appear like little sparks of interest, and exist through the composer's exposition of artistic, skilled and beautifully conceived movement ideas which stand out as such to the onlooker.

Some of the means by which climaxes or highlights can be achieved in movement are illustrated in Table 4 overleaf.

TABLE 4
SOME IDEAS ON HOW CLIMAX OR HIGHLIGHT MIGHT BE ACHIEVED

ACTION

1. Special emphasis on one or a few actions within the motif through:
a) repetition
b) enlargement by means of development
c) defined by stillness before or after the action/s

2. Change in action content

3. Interesting development or variation through addition of action content

QUALITY

1. Sudden or subtle change of qualities

2. Build up in force or time or both

   Sudden accents-short continuous dynamic passages

3. Repetition of rhythmic pattern-change of rhythmic pattern

4. Contrast in flow

CLIMAX OR HIGHLIGHT through

SPACE

1. Sudden or subtle change or contrast in:
a) amount of space used,
b) placing in space,
c) focus in space,
d) space pattern – size, level direction, pathway

2. Special enlargement or development of the spatial aspects of the motif

RELATIONSHIP

1. Variation or contrast of group relationship

2. Addition in number moving
Subtraction in number moving

3. Particular juxta-positioning of the movements within the motifs, phrases or sections

Proportion and Balance

These are complementary elements of construction. Proportion refers to the size and magnitude of each part in relation to the whole, and balance refers to the equilibrium of content within each of these proportionate parts and the whole.

The proportion of one part of a dance in relation to its other parts has to be right. Equal proportioning of parts may become too boring. It is all too easy to go on developing for too long with one motif or statement or conversely, make too little of a section of movement content thereby losing its significance through lack of repetition. Each part of a dance should be only as long as is necessary. There is no easy answer for a perfect proportion of parts in any dance. It is an intuitive feeling for 'rightness' that guides the use of this element of construction.

Similar comments can be made in reference to balance. Here the composer must be aware of the balance which exists in his *choice* of movement content within one part of his dance in relation to his choice in another. Within the range of material that the composer deems suitable for the total dance, it is important to consider the proportionate use so that the whole is balanced. A beginning 'packed with delights' and then trailing away to an uninteresting end is unbalanced, whereas a dance which has its contrasts, climaxes or highlights, repetitions and variations in movement content spaced out throughout its duration may well be judged as a balanced form and should succeed in sustaining interest. The composer's aim is to achieve equilibrium of parts so that a unity becomes apparent. For instance, the gentle flowing parts of the dance should not be made insignificant in relation to the strong dominant parts. The section of the dance performed by a soloist should stand as significant in juxtaposition with the section in which a large group performs. All parts must enhance the idea and be inseparable from the whole.

In a more specific sense, the proportion element of construction could refer to how many dancers are performing and the proportionate divisions within the number. The balance element could refer to where they are in relation to each other and the space. (Some detail on this is included in Methods of Construction III.) It is important that proportion of numbers is relevant and enhances the dance idea, and that these must change in order to keep it an interesting feature. Similarly, the balance and placing of the groups in relation to each other has expressive significance. The arrangement and placing of dancers and props in the stage space is governed by a need for symmetric or asymmetric balancing which is determined by the composer's treatment of the theme. The composer should also consider the proportionate use of the stage space to give a balanced effect within the environment.

Transition

The composer must use this element of construction to link all the parts and effectively create a whole. Transitions are very important and perhaps the most difficult aspects of the composition.

There are no set ways of making transitions from one part of a dance to another. The composer usually works on these in an intuitive way. Finding an answer to a movement problem can only be achieved by moving through all the possible avenues until it feels and looks right.

Transitions can be very short or quite long in time. Indeed a transition from one part to another may be effected by merely *holding still* in a body position before moving into the new part. This has the effect of holding on to something for a second or two whilst an impression is formed by the audience before changing the subject. Or, the transition may be made as a *hesitation* between movements or phrases or as *anticipation* of movement to follow—for example, a lean of the body into a direction before actually travelling on that pathway. Transitions hold each part together by bridging and, therefore, help to create the overall rhythmical framework. The longer transition, lasting perhaps as long as *phrase*, usually acts as a link between sections.

The subtle transitions from one position to another, and the more obvious transitions from one section of the dance to another, all play an important tying-together role. Movement tied to movement should be logical, clear and, above all, appear easily performed. Movements of a transition between sections should, perhaps, have a lingering flavour of the preceding section and act as an introductory passage to the succeeding section.

Logical Development

Logical development becomes apparent by virtue of repetition, climax, transition, contrast and variety in the dance. When we speak of logical development, we refer to the natural growth of the dance from its beginning to its end. If something is logical it also has meaning and 'raison d'etre' throughout its existence. The beginning of the dance starts a line of thought for the onlooker and from this, ideas offshoot in many directions, while all retain a common thread. The common thread is the basis upon which logical development depends, and is more than just the idea, story or motivational stimulus of the dance. The common thread is initiated through the beginning motif which is a *movement interpretation* of the motivation or idea behind the dance. This movement interpretation has an identity in terms of action, qualities, space and perhaps relationships. The rest of the dance, or a part of the dance, discloses more of this identity through repetition, variation and contrast. The pursuit of form created from the identity of the foundational motifs determines logical development. In this way all the movements appear relevant and part of the growth of the dance. The climaxes are in the right places and have the right kind of initiation to fulfil their purpose. The whole leads perfectly to its end which seems right as an outcome. Not inevitable, but right. In fact the end of a dance is probably the most important part. If the end fails—the dance fails.

To summarise: logical development of the dance ensures unification whereby each part is linked to the common thread through the composer's movement interpretation of the idea. If the constructional elements of motifs, developments, variations, contrasts, climaxes or highlights, and above all transitions are successfully employed, then the dance appears to have logical development which in turn produces unity.

Unity

This is the overall constructional element. The final shape that emerges when the dance is over is realised through unity. To make an analogy; if all the parts fit into the jigsaw puzzle it finally produces a whole picture within its round or square frame. The *movement content* with its inherent meaning and the way in which the *constructional elements* have been employed form the pieces of the jigsaw and its overall shape or dance form (e.g. Ternary form) forms the frame. The pieces knitted together become unified within the frame and also form the frame which produces unity. If even one piece is missing or does not fit then the whole never becomes a whole and unity is lost.

The dance composer must aim for unity. To understand how it is reached in a dance requires a good deal of experience and artistic awareness, but it can be recognised by laymen and even by children. Somehow a good dance is appreciated as an entity which has meaning and significance beyond the scope of its pieces. A dance which has the quality of unity is likely to be successful.

METHODS OF
CONSTRUCTION VI.

Style*
Understanding the Term 'Style'. Factors Affecting the Style of a Dance. How to Stylise a Dance.

Understanding the Term 'Style'

In dance, the terms style and technique can mean one and the same thing because the word technique often means the content of the idiom, not merely how it is manipulated/ presented. Thus we have ballet, jazz, contemporary techniques which produce these particular styles. For some, use of the word genre to describe the idiom or type of dance—ballet, jazz, contemporary—provides a solution since each can be articulated in many stylistic flavours. For example, a contemporary dance might be labelled jazzy in style, balletic or neo-classical, ethnic or as having a particular social dance flavour.

The word technique is also used in most dance contexts when discussing physical skill and, to a dancer, technique means acquiring skill through attending class, exercising the body and practising movements to achieve perfection. The class invariably is taken in one technique as opposed to another —i.e. to become skilled in ballet one goes to ballet classes. So, at class level, the words technique and style often do mean the same thing. Genre is not yet a word in common usage.

It is interesting to study how new techniques, or changes of emphasis in traditional techniques, form particular styles. All choreographers try to invent new styles and even if a traditional style is used, rather than merely rearranging the pre-scribed content, the choreographer will probably take elements from the traditional style and embrace them within a style more relevant to the choreographer's own time.

Balanchine, as an example of a master classicist, abstracted the pure classical syntax of movement from ballet and developed it into modern-formalism. This term describes a style which has been created through a process of abstraction. From

* This text is largely derived from a lecture delivered by Jacqueline Smith at the Summer Conference of the National Association of Teachers in Further and Higher Education in association with the British Society of Aesthetics in 1982 and subsequently printed in the 'Dance Section Collected Conference Papers' (NATFHE 1983).

the traditional theatrical spectacle of ballet, Balanchine abstracted the 'bare-bones' austerity of ballet essence. In exploring the essence of ballet, Balanchine concentrated on the movement itself and particularly concerned himself with the phenomenon of grace. Technique was the means by which his dancers achieved the essential grace which, for Balanchine, was the essence of ballet. His particular ways of moving into and out of ballet positions and linking of movements created his style—the Balanchine style relevant to his time. His manipulation of the standardised technical elements of ballet was the outcome of a mixture of experiences—those early in his life in St. Petersburg and with the Diaghilev company, those connected with twentieth century modern expressionist dance styles and those connected with modern art in general and music in particular. Furthermore, the general style of American dancers with its broad, expansive and energetic characteristics similarly influenced his movement repertoire. All of these influences and doubtless others, became absorbed and structured into a coherent Balanchine style.

Balanchine's ballets are prime examples of the changes in emphasis in ballet technique in that legs are extended very high, there is an accent on line and fluency, the torso is used to tip the body into and out of balances and the aspect of body design or shape is an apparent focus throughout his work to generate the quality of grace for its own sake. The style, therefore, *creates* the expression of grace, the technique or content with its emphasis on line, shape, balance, etc., and the choreographic form with an emphasis on order, harmony and a pleasingly unified appearance, create the style of modern-formalism. Modern, because it is a twentieth century development of a traditional style and formalism, because it focuses on form and movement for its own sake.

Factors Affecting Style

From the above brief discussion of Balanchine's style, it would appear relevant, in summary, to say that style is culturally and historically defined but, in dance as in other arts it also has much to do with the technique employed. Graham's work is a clear example of how technique forms the basis of style and expression in dance and how this is formulated out of a need to find ways of expressing in a manner relevant to the time and place in which the art form finds itself.

Martha Graham's technique evolved first as a means of:

expressing personal feelings and national identity through recognisable prototypes of character and movement and the abstraction of those feelings to a more cosmic level through the use of symbol, myth and psychoanalytic exploration.

(Seigel 1979)

This stylised naturalism was typical of the 1930s period when Graham first started to choreograph. In a Graham dance people make statements. Most often these are dramatic and powerful. To effect this Graham's theatre dance style is distinguished by its unnaturalness. As Seigel says, 'Graham has always tried to formalise natural impulses, to abstract human feelings into a set expressive language'. This procedure was common in the 1930s when Freudian theory encouraged artists to explore new ways of expressing human feelings. As Jowitt states:

Graham likened herself, at a primitive stage in her development, to the dancer in a primitive culture . . . She would start from scratch, concentrating on the pulse of the body, on the rhythmic action of the foot against the ground, and articulate the head, arms and hands as her work evolved . . . breath was crucial—not so much everyday even-rhythmed breathing, but the gasp, the sob, the slow sigh of relief, and the ways in which these—heightened and abstracted—could affect the dancer's muscles and skeleton. Her theory of 'contraction and release' was built on the act of inhaling and exhaling. The dancer, whether sitting, standing, kneeling or lying down, caves in as if suddenly hit with a blow to the center of her body. But 'caves in' is the wrong term if that implies any relaxation of tension . . . As Graham developed her technique, a contraction might hit the dancer sideways, make her twist, spiral, or be spun to the floor. It might attack percussively then deepen slowly, resonating throughout her body. But always, no matter how drastic the fall, there is release, a rise, an advance, an inhalation. The dancer waits—poised, charged—for the next crisis. (pp. 164, 166; 1988)

Ideas like these created very individual styles of dance movement. Certainly, the Graham technique is idiosyncratic and as demanding and unnatural as classical ballet. However, the style and kind of expression most characteristic of Graham's work, seem no longer relevant to today's choreographers so the contemporary techniques used in dance works, though frequently derived from Graham's technique, have changed. It is interesting to note the similarity between ballet and contemporary dance here, in that it is common practice to take Graham classes, learning the Graham specified expressive language and perfecting a whole range of unnatural movement content and yet, in the performance of choreographers' works, never to use these movements in their original form. Hence, we see a definite division between the style of what is taught in technique class and what is required on stage. (It is acknowledged that the body instrument is superbly tuned and prepared for any dance co-ordination by virtue of the practice of Graham technique, but if the term technique refers to content for dance, the actual movement content is no longer relevantly expressive for today's choreographers.) Yet, the style of Graham's work remains, in essence, the hallmark of most of the contemporary theatre dance available to us. The styles of Graham, Cunningham and a few other early modern dance artists have become integrated and generalised to serve the needs of present day choreographers.

This generalised contemporary dance style includes movements emphasising the use of the torso, feet in parallel, strict concern for body design and spatial design, movements of isolated parts of the body as well as the whole, emphasis on the pelvic region and the centre initiating and causing momentum, tension between up and down, floor-work and extensive variations of qualities and phrasing. The dance composer, through study of contemporary dance works on video or preferably in live theatre settings, will absorb the flavour of this generalised contemporary dance style and employ it as a basic stylistic source for his/her own dances.

Another important feature of the generalised style in mainstream dance choreography is the use of symbolic action embedded in a unified whole. This can be illustrated by reference to Jiri Kylian's work. In his dances based upon ideas the symbols are not literal and referential. The image is abstract and subtle in meaning. But his style of symbolising a theme is also very much integrated with his style of forming a dance and it is this aspect of his choreography which is masterful. One becomes delighted by the build-up, integration and development of motifs, the inventive way in which they are repeated within intricate patternings, the excitement of choreographic devices, such as canon, perfectly placed to make important moments stay in one's mind long after the dance is over, the intricacy, fluency and grace of the couples weaving around, over, through, towards and away from each other creating particularly pleasing spatial and rhythmic nuances. These are some of the ways in which Kylian's personal style becomes evident and some of the reasons why his works also, like Balanchine's, can be labelled as modern-formalism.

There is a recognisable look to Kylian's work as there is to Balanchine's and Graham's. Kylian, like other choreographers, attempts to move away from any such trademark. He said 'I prefer to think I didn't have a style. I like to change my ways from ballet to ballet but, of course, you cannot avoid your own handwriting' (reported by Anna Kisselgoff writing in the New York Times 1979).

So far then, in the contemporary dance context we have the current generalised dance technique style, the ways in which ideas are presented symbolically with a concentration on stripping away the dramatic literal gesture content to create a subtle hints on the idea, and an emphasis on the form aspects of composition, all contributing to the overall style of dances. Added to this list, the following factors also affect style.

Each theme has stylistic properties intrinsic to it. For example, in Bruce's 'Berlin Requiem' 1982, we see the styles of the 30s dance forms, characteristic poses and behaviours of the bar-frequenting social group, amalgamated with some movement characteristics of the films of the period. To embody the expression, these stylistc aspects of the theme are inextricably interwoven with a contemporary dance style and approaches to choreography as listed above. But, since Bruce has done the amalgamating and weaving of the parts into a unified whole, the result carries a powerful Bruce signature.

Hence, it appears that the style and expression of a dance work is likely to emerge as a compound of several elements, each of which have boundaries. The technique and kind (genre) of dance sets one boundary, the motivation or theme sets another boundary. Added to these we have the personal style of the choreographer pervading the work. This comes over as a personal interpretation and way of using the technique, together with a personal interpretation of the idea and the conventions and meanings associated with it. So, we have the possibility of style within style, within style.

Yet another stylistic boundary derives from the current views on dance as a theatre art and the choreographer's attitude towards these. Clearly, both Bruce and Kylian are what might be labelled 'mainstream' choreographers—they use highly skilled dancers, they generally have themes to dance about, they create symbols abstracting the essence of the idea. Kylian concentrates on sheer dance quality, the theme instrumental to this, while Bruce gives greater emphasis to the emotional impact of the theme. But both aim for unity of form. They present the dance works so that the audiences can enjoy the intrinsic qualities of good dancing, line, shape, pattern, dynamic contrasts etc. Kylian emphasises formalism and the physical side of it, Bruce emphasises expressionism, but clearly both adhere to the mainstream view of dance.

Contrary to this, we have the post-modern or new dance exponents who have formulated different views of dance as art. Here, the outcome is dependent upon how they see dance: as unconnected or fragmented movements in time and space, or as mathematically organised movement in time and space, or as natural everyday action for its own sake, or as spontaneous response to commands or improvised movement of others, or as informed happenings, or as exposure of social behaviours through realistic physical contact and body language which might otherwise be confined to private relationships (e.g. 'DV8'). However, these are not the only characteristics which result in these choreographers being collectively called post-moderns. In addition, they share characteristics such as the manner of working choreographically—by experimentation with little concern for rules or conventions—and the movement content—mostly natural, relaxed and showing little concern for shape, placement or focus in space and technically complex patterns of movement. These are some of the distinguishing features of the post-modern style/genre.

How to Stylise a Dance

It is obvious, then, that the complexity of the concept of style demands that a composer understands what is involved in stylising a dance and that it cannot be left to chance if the dance is going to make an impact and 'stand the test of time'. While these might appear grandiose ideals for a student composer, it is always necessary to aim for originality if the created dance is to be valued. Copying the style of a known choreographer can be a useful learning process but ultimately, even if a dance is composed 'in the style of . . .', it should bear the distinctive signature of the composer. No two people have exactly the same backgrounds, even if trained at the same time and in the same place they will perceive it differently because of their own different experiences. Moreover, interpretation of themes, use of techniques in movement and compositional form will vary from person to person. This is what is so special about art—each person's work is distinctive. Style is one of the features which makes for this distinction but it is also influenced by the cultural and artistic practices of particular times and places. It is the understanding of these practices that the student composer needs to develop so that the dances composed achieve both artistic relevance and originality.

The range and complexity of expression in dance today demands a complex mixing of tried and tested techniques and styles and a constant search for new ones. For example, a theme may require a social/contemporary dance style such as Twyla Tharp's 'Sinatra Suite (1977), a neo-classical style such as Jiri Kylian's 'Sinfonietta' (1979), a physical theatre/contact improvisation style such as DV8's 'Dead Dreams of Monochrome Men' (1988), an ethnically influenced style such as Christopher Bruce's 'Ghost Dances' (1981). Whatever the theme the composer needs to research all aspects of its time/ place i.e. the cultural characteristics, and search for the most appropriate technique/content and choreographic approach to express it. To do this it might be helpful to study ways in which the theme has been expressed before, if it has, so that the composer's choice of style is informed.

An ability to make such decisions implies a vast knowledge of techniques and styles and, of course, student composers do not often have more than one technique in their repertoire with its intrinsic style, be it ballet, contemporary or jazz, for example. In education, there is insufficient time to train young dancers to achieve mastery of skill in even one technique and it would be wrong to do this anyway because it immediately limits the style and kinds of expression to those which that particular technique can articulate. All techniques have such limitations.

It would seem that, in an ideal world, pupils in school and

college should come to understand the significant differences in expression in a number of tried and tested techniques and styles so that they may selectively employ the right combinations of these in their own creative endeavours. Resource-based teaching/learning, the subject of the next section in this book, is in my view the best way forward. A study of current and past repertoire of dance art works in the composer's own culture and outside it too has to be the means towards the end of developing an understanding of style and how to stylise a dance. This is how musicians learn about style—through listening to, studying and playing renowned pieces. Dance composers too need to work in this way—watch, study and perform snippets from dance works choreographed by professionals.

Section III

RESOURCE-BASED TEACHING/ LEARNING OF DANCE COMPOSITION

Resource-based Teaching/Learning. Resource-based Teaching —Kinds of Learning Experiences. Using Resources to Teach Dance Composition.

Resource-based Teaching/Learning

Resource-based teaching/learning, in a general sense, has been around for a very long time especially in primary education. It is the term given to situations in which pupils are set tasks or set themselves tasks which lead them to explore and search for information or answers to problems from a range of source materials, often found in the resource centre of the school. The teacher has the role of catalyst, adviser and manager in identifying what is to be learned and the resources which might be employed, but largely, the learning is pupil directed. It is common practice to use such approaches in project work which might integrate areas of work such as a study of the natural world linked with historical and geographical perspectives. Here, the pupils might need to search through written material in books, magazines, newspapers etc., watch film clips, look at pictures, go outside and observe particular phenomena etc. Most subject areas have large banks of resources which can be employed in this way.

In the arts too, this kind of resource-based teaching could effectively be used to research a topic. For example, a number of works choreographed by different people could be used as references in the study of style or in the study of a type of form such as narrative, or for the purposes of studying how the same theme can be treated differently. If this sort of work is to be undertaken by pupils in self-directed projects, there is need for resource banks of books, videos, theatre programmes, reviews, recorded interviews with choreographers etc. But dance education has been rather slow in developing such an

89

approach. Perhaps this can be explained with reference to the relatively poor status that dance has had in the overall curriculum which might result in an under funding and a lack of resources. But, in the dance composition context, a more likely explanation, is the reluctance of teachers to change from the traditional approach of the teacher setting the whole class a task, based on some form of stimulus and moving round to help individuals or groups to come to some expected solution, rather than developing a more student centred and resource based methodology.

It might not be surprising, however, that, having shifted from the school-based Laban model which made little or no reference to dance in the outside world, to that described as the dance as art model which is quite obviously tied to the theatre dance context, teachers who take their pupils to the theatre and have them view videos believe themselves to be employing a resource-based teaching approach. Indeed it would be very difficult to teach dance as an art form without reference to public examples of the art form. It would be like never considering concerts—live or recorded, art galleries or books containing masterpieces in paint or other media, or literary work, poems and plays as part of the arts curriculum. Hence, dance teachers too, through theatre visits, workshops with dance artists, and setting classes to view videos of dance works, have responded to the need to make reference to theatre dance as exemplification of the art form. However, this is just a beginning—a scratching of the surface of resource based teaching/learning.

As resources, art works are very special. They cannot be likened to reference books, objects of nature, etc. Each one is unique, conveying its own meanings. Each has its own aesthetic qualities. Each is worth getting to know and understand for its own sake as a source for artistic and aesthetic experience. Properly employed as resources, art works involve the learner both affectively and cognitively. This is the speciality of the arts, the only area of the curriculum to involve pupils in both feeling and thinking. Professionally wrought art works have the function of taking the perceiver beyond his/her private domain towards understanding more about human feelings and about the world in general. Consequently, coming to know dances as art works is a first priority for dance teachers employing a resource-based teaching methodology. This is more important than any amount of use of dance works as reference resources to aid development of knowledge and understanding of concepts external to the works of art themselves. However, in the dance teaching context to date, resources are inadequate and methods of using them to further artistic and aesthetic education are not yet publicly proposed.

The following text provides a start in offering some methods in which dance works can be used as resources but teachers of dance should continue to demand resources, especially videos of dance works together with packs of teaching materials to accompany them.

Resource-based Teaching—Kinds of Learning Experience

There are to my mind two kinds of approach in delivery of the curriculum in which resource-based teaching methods can feature. Both aim towards the same thing i.e. self-directed activities leading to greater understanding, knowledge and improved skills in the learner. The first method will be known to the reader as the thematic approach, in that a common theme links subject areas together. Here, dance may be at the centre, that is the initial impetus or wellspring of the project outcome which might be illustrated thus:

Or, dance could be one of the subjects on the outer ring, another aspect of the curriculum forming the focus. This approach is most often employed in the primary sector, but within the many new arts faculties in secondary schools, and because of the restrictiveness of single arts' subject time on the National Curriculum, there is going to be a growth in this kind of inter-relationship and therefore further opportunities for both a thematic and resource-based teaching approach.

To reiterate, resource-based teaching by definition requires that pupils learn from resources and employ them as starting points or exemplars upon which to base their own work. The resource may well provide a theme but this is not the only feature of it employed for teaching purposes. Rather, the teacher should use it as fully as possible so that pupils develop knowledge and understanding of it per se and the subject area of which it is an example i.e. a dance work informing pupils about the art form of dance. Taking the theme as a means of providing links between different resources/experiences is a teaching device to help pupils apply concepts in different situations and see relationships between things. Hence, in the arts, resource-based teaching linked with a thematic approach has three objectives:

a) to provide pupils with as many learning situations as possible so that they come to know more about and 'get inside' the resource/art work for its own sake;

b) to provide pupils some means of learning about the art form through the resource as exemplification; and

c) to provide pupils opportunities to study and come to know more about the theme.

For example, a snippet from a dance video resource used in an attempt to develop the pupils' artistic/aesthetic perceptions of it as an art work and of dance as an art form, could also be employed as a theme in other subjects/areas of the curriculum. For younger pupils, the opening sequence of Jiri Kylian's 'L'Enfant et les Sortilèges' (1984), in which a young boy is depicted as angry and bad tempered, provides a good means of initiating work from a dance starting point. With repeated reference to the snippet of video, each time encouraging the pupils to perceive different aspects, the kinds of movements and qualities used and the expression conveyed, the use of music, the relationship of the dancer to the objects and people on the stage, pupils not only learn how to view in greater depth, but learn more about making dances too. At the same time, a great deal of work across a range of the curriculum can be generated on the theme of anger as a mood: language work in discussion of the feelings of anger that the pupils themselves have experienced, drama to explore further what kind of feeling anger is, art work to represent this in colour and/or shape, poems to express their own views on anger, music compositions to go with the dance outcome and, of course, the pupils' own 'Anger' dance itself, having studied, critically evaluated and learned from Kylian's presentation of the theme in dance form. This planned use of a resource as a central reference point determining the type and range of activities to be experienced by the pupils, can be said to be a thematic approach in teaching employing a resource-based method which encompasses pupil-directed activity.

The second approach in delivery of curriculum content in which a resource-based teaching methodology can be beneficial is where the activities emanating from the resource provide in-depth understanding/appreciation of the resource as an exemplification of a subject i.e. in this case—the art of dance. In other words there is an inward focus towards the subject itself and the teacher's primary aim is that the pupils come to know and understand more about the subject through a thorough use of the resource. Any recourse to other subject areas serves only to illuminate further the subject area being studied.

This discipline-based approach is perhaps more likely to be found in secondary schools where subjects do not interrelate in any planned way. A piece of professional choreography is most frequently employed as the resource in dance, all of the activities emanating from or making reference to this choreography. Pupils might explore the theme of the dance through discussion, looking at pictures, reading and responding to poems on the same theme etc. They would come to understand the feelings, style and meanings in the movements of the dance by guided viewing and perhaps learning and performing some short sections from it. They might utilise the pre-planned worksheets and view the dance several times to develop an appreciation of the choreographic form of the dance. They might answer the questions on another worksheet about the accompaniment, costumes and design. They could take some of the movements as starting points for their own composition on the same or a similar theme or even alter certain aspects of them to utilise them in a different choreographic context. They could be taught and perform a technical study in the same style of the piece. Also they might study this work in comparison with works of another choreographer. They might study reviews of the work and contextualise it historically and culturally in relation to other works.

The following illustrates some of the ways in which a resource can be used within a discipline-based learning context.

DISCIPLINE/RESOURCE-BASED TEACHING OF DANCE COMPOSITION

Resource = a professionally choreographed and performed dance

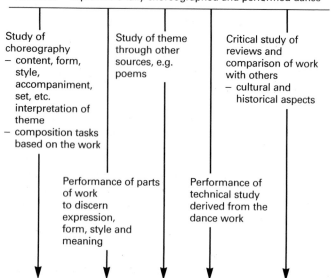

Study of choreography
– content, form, style, accompaniment, set, etc. interpretation of theme
– composition tasks based on the work

Study of theme through other sources, e.g. poems

Critical study of reviews and comparison of work with others
– cultural and historical aspects

Performance of parts of work to discern expression, form, style and meaning

Performance of technical study derived from the dance work

Leads to in-depth artistic/aesthetic appreciation of the dance work and a greater understanding/knowledge and expertise in dance composition

In both the above cases the resources bring the public world of dance into the experience of the pupil. Acquaintance knowledge derived from use of ready-made dance art works feeds the young learner composer in a direct and significant way. Excitement and feeling generated from enjoyment of an art work seem somehow to enrich the learner and influence the outcomes of his/her own compositions. Such enjoyment will not be experienced, however, unless the perceiver has learned how to perceive the nuances of expression, form, style etc. in the work. A carefully planned set of experiences with the resource/s is most important if artistic and aesthetic enjoyment and learning from this are the aim.

Theatre visits constitute an essential part of dance education and most dance teachers take pupils out, have dance companies visit the school or both. Sometimes pupils should just see professional dance works for enjoyment alone without 'doing any work' connected with the experience. But, at other times students would benefit in having their perceptions guided. For example, the dance appreciation tasks in Section V headed 'Before going to see the Performance' and 'After the Performance', most of which derive from the Ballet Rambert 'Dance Appreciation Teaching Units'*, are designed in the:

> hope that pupils might become more able to express some of the ideas and feelings that they experience when they view dance works. It is not intended to make the pupils see dances in any particular way. Rather, we think it is preferable to offer them a frame of reference so that they can confidently organise what they see and feel into meaningful experiences. *It is our aim to structure perception without narrowly directing it.* To do this we have posed questions and tasks which demand that pupils recall some of the expressive, sensory and formal qualities in the dance works . . . this classification of aesthetic qualities forms a valuable frame of reference by which appreciation of dance works might be guided.
>
> (J. M. Smith and S. Newman 1978)

The '*Before going to see the Performance*' unit provides pupils with tasks which draw attention to aesthetic/artistic qualities which might be found in dance works. Practice in using structured tasks in imagined dance contexts will perhaps enable students to direct their own perceptions to aesthetic/artistic qualities while viewing live dance performances. Task 2, for example, requires that they use knowledge about movement and meaning (Section I—The Material Content in this book), in imagining expressive qualities which might be found in movements. In discerning such meanings, tasks 3–5 concentrate attention on intrinsic qualities in the movements themselves and require pupils to find words to describe them and task 6 asks them to respond similarly to costume and design elements.

* These *Dance Appreciation Teaching Units for Schools and Colleges* were written for Ballet Rambert by the author of this book with Stephen Newman who was the education officer of the company in 1978.

The 'After going to see the Performance' unit aims that pupils recall the perceptions of aesthetic/artistic qualities they experienced when watching the dance work/s. This sort of work helps to reinforce the knowledge that pupils are gaining in practical dance experiences. For example, task 4 asks that they recall elements of dance construction which they may well have employed themselves in composing their own dances (Methods of Construction V in this book). It also asks them to recall the feelings that they had while engaged in viewing the work. This is very important of course, if the resource is to be enjoyed as a feeling experience as well as an example from which much about dance can be learned.

Resource-based teaching derived from theatre visits and the like, is an important means towards the end of pupils coming to appreciate dance art works and learning from these total and absorbing aesthetic experiences. However, school/college based work employing dance works as resources towards more specific objectives such as developing the pupils' abilities to compose dances, is likely to feature more regularly in a dance education programme. Of course, such work also develops a greater awareness of the intrinsic qualities in theatre dance and provides a knowledge base upon which pupils can critically evaluate professionally choreographed dances.

Using Resources to Teach Dance Composition

To demonstrate how a video resource can be employed to teach dance composition, a set of assignments from Section V is discussed in detail here. The resource employed is the publicly available video of Christopher Bruce's 'Intimate Pages' (1984). The first three phrases are studied in depth in the tasks outlined but the whole work should be viewed and discussed/ studied in different ways to deepen and extend the students' knowledge of it as an artistic/aesthetic whole.

The tasks are designed to be student centred, perhaps carried out by some groups while others are working on some other projects.

Activity A: Small group discussion—no more than five.

Video snippet—the beginning phrases up until the woman has stroked the man's head with her right hand. This should be made available in isolation from the rest of the dance work and as an easily repeatable video resource.

Question 1. Can you find two phrases and the beginning of a third phrase? What starts and ends each phrase?

Question 2. What sort of feelings are the man and the woman expressing?

Write down your answers to present to others.

These questions demand that the pupils study the time design, understand how it has been constructed (see Methods of Construction IV) and how it contributes to the expression of the ideas they think the snippet conveys.

Activity B: Study of choreography and practical composition task in twos. Video snippet—same as above viewed several times as required.

1. Describe and list the spatial relationships between the dancers (e.g. facing, at the side of, on) in:

   a) phrase 1 and   b) phrase 2

   Is there a difference in the relationships shown in the two phrases?

2. Describe the changes of speed you see. Why do you think the choreographer uses these?

3. Duo task—practical composition:

   Choose one of the following ideas:

   an argument—forbidden love—despondence

   Discuss the meanings you wish to convey. Use at least three of the duo relationships you listed in 1) above as a basis for a short dance sequence.

Here the pupils' perceptions are directed towards the content and the kinds of meanings it conveys to them. They would be expected to employ the terminology used to describe spatial and relationship aspects in the first activity and qualitative aspects of speed in the second. A range of words should be encouraged especially in respect of describing the feelings that the content expresses and how it expresses them. In discerning the differences in the two phrases they would be expected to note the repetitions, developments and contrasts apparent in the content and be guided to see that the motif at the beginning

97

is developed and extended in the second phrase but that the meanings differ because of different spatial, relationship and time changes.

The choreographic task to create a duo on a similar theme, gives pupils opportunity to apply the above perceptions appropriately in their own work and yet gives them imaginative freedom to interpret the theme in their way. A ready-made bank of movement ideas as a starting point inspires rather than limits creativity. To work from 'givens' towards originality is an essential aim of resource-based teaching of dance composition. This idea is endorsed by Best (1985) who says:

> To be creative requires a grasp of the criteria of validity and value in the activity in question. Originality is given its sense only against a background of the traditional . . . imagination is imagination only in so far as it operates within limits. (pp. 78/9)

(Further discussion on this can be found in the next section headed 'Standing Back From the Process: The Composer's Freedom').

Activity C: Refining the composition and practising performance of it.

Video snippet—as above—view as many times as required.

1. Watch how the dancers link their movements to make the phrases fluid and continuous.
    — Watch also for the pauses.
    — Make your own composition clear in its use of continuity and pauses and then practise it paying particular attention to continuity and pauses in conveying the meanings.

2. Watch the video again.
    — Are the pauses dead still? If not, what keeps the dance movement going at these points?
    — Practise your duo again working on the pauses to make them 'live and breathe'.

3. Have your duo videoed and then discuss with your partner ways in which your performance could be improved.
    — Write a self-assessment on the composition and on your own performance in the duo.

Here, the students are led towards perceiving the qualitative details in Bruce's choreography. Their appreciation of the qualities of continuity and stillness as important features conveying meanings is thus enhanced and then applied in critically evaluating their own work. In this way, the superb example of Bruce's 'Intimate Pages' feeds and enriches the students' own composition. Moreover, they should come to understand that the quality of performance can make or mar the meaning in the dance.

There are many, many features of this one work which could be employed in activities such as those outlined above. In fact almost all of the content in this book could be exemplified in 'Intimate Pages' and many composition tasks could be derived from it. However, it is important that any one dance is not over used as a means of learning how to compose. The teacher should be sensitive in judging just how deeply pupils can delve into a work and how long they can stay with it. Clearly, the central objectives of resource-based teaching have failed to be met if pupils get bored or start disliking the art work. If activities are varied enough, however, pupils can stay with one work for several dance lessons without losing the interest and excitement of the first viewing. Indeed, it is often the case that the longer students stay with a work the more they get to enjoy it. Obviously, the teacher knows best and may well choose to employ a range of different dance works in order to study other aspects of composition. But it should be remembered that the most important aim for resource-based teaching in the arts is that pupils get fully acquainted with and have feelings for the art works themselves.

It is impossible to describe in a text such as this the extent of artistic and aesthetic learning that could take place through such student centred learning experiences. Resource-based teaching involving use of dance works in ways described above and in Section V of this text, is an important methodology for dance in education. More than any other method, it successfully integrates the three strands—composing, performing and viewing dances, the conceptual basis of the dance as art model.

Section IV

STANDING BACK FROM THE PROCESS: THE COMPOSER'S FREEDOM

The process of composing a dance varies with each person who attempts it, and no-one can set out rules or methods of progression which can be followed in order to achieve guaranteed success.

When the composer is at work there is constant influence exerted from the inter-relationship of his/her:

1) imagination and intuition,
2) knowledge of movement material,
3) knowledge of methods of construction, and
4) acquaintance knowledge of form, style and meaning in the aesthetic realm which has been gained through experience of seeing other people's dances and art works in forms other than dance.

Until now, this book has been concerned mainly with the areas 2 and 3 above and to some extent 4 has been discussed in the section on resource-based teaching. To consider the inter-relationship further it becomes necessary to attempt more detail of 1 and 4.

Imagination and Intuition

The fact that the composer's imagination and intuition are active during the creation of a dance cannot be disputed. These are elusive qualities and to discuss when they function, and even what they are, is very difficult indeed. The following ideas on some possible roles that imagination and intuition might play in the composition of a dance, are based upon the experience of making dances and discussion with many students both during and after the process of composing.

Imagination

Clearly the dance composer cannot function without using imagination. One of the definitions offered in Webster's Dictionary (1966) is:

> . . . the ability or gift of forming conscious ideas or mental images especially for the purpose of artistic or intellectual creation.

A composer has complete freedom of imagination until he/she has decided on the idea for a dance. Sometimes, this can be a difficult decision if the imagination is fired by many alternative ideas. In choosing a theme, the inexperienced composer is often unaware of the pitfalls when he/she tries—unsuccessfully—to translate great epics or very involved and intricate plots into dance form. He/she imagines these complex dances, and attempts to interpret them without any real knowledge or awareness of the technical problems which need to be addressed. A skilled dance composer has acquired this knowledge, and understands that it is an integral part of the craft. Through the experience of trial and error, a creative person endeavouring to compose dances gradually learns that knowledge of the limitations of the art form disciplines imagination to that which is possible.

The Imagination and the Composer's Initial Reaction to the Stimulus

Material Content

On hearing a lively piece of music the composer, spontaneously or through meditation, consciously recalls movements which pertain to the quality of liveliness. This response may occur simultaneously with movement if the composer improvises immediately with the music, or it may occur solely within the thought of the composer while listening to the music.

The composer's initial reaction to the stimulus thus evokes certain conscious ideas or mental images but these do not come from 'out of the blue', for as Redfern (1973) states:

> To be imaginative in the aesthetic realm demands knowledge and understanding of the standards and techniques peculiar to the art form in question.

The conscious recall of suitable movements for communication of liveliness occurs within the imagination of the composer. He/she imagines a dancer or dancers performing movements which he/she *knows* (knowledge) and which are within the range of acceptable vocabulary to depict the mood (understanding of the standards).

The Dance Form

During or after this initial response to the music, and as a result of it, the composer may imagine a dance outcome. The outcome, whether an entire framework or only a small part, continues to guide the composer's movement response to the stimulus. The outcome might, for example, be seen to grow to a height in the middle when the lively dance would contain extravagant jumps, turns, rolls and leaps. It might also be imagined to have a final leap which exits from the stage. The composer, with this in mind, then begins to manipulate material to fit these conscious images, and thus starts composing.

The Imagination During Composition

Material Content

The composer continues to search for movements from his/her repertoire which are deemed suitable, and tries to make them as original (imaginative) as possible. Perhaps this is achieved by altering the more commonly employed movement characteristics, such as, size, level, direction, part of body utilised, qualitative content and gesture. It is understandable that the composer should want to aim for originality in the sense of doing something that has not been done before. It is also understandable that he/she should wish to move away from conventional movement towards a form which is unique and his/her own. But the movements:

> . . . can hardly be counted as original or imaginative if they occur without reference to existing practices, and without the understanding and deliberate intent which make a 'differing form' possible.

> Redfern (1973)

This reinforces the comment made previously, that, however original, the vocabulary must be recognisable to be successful. It can be open to many interpretations but these should be within a certain realm of ideas. We all look for imaginative or original movement material and evaluate dances with this as a criterion. The composer should set out with this aim. It may be that the dance demands to be stated simply, but the simplest movement content can be presented imaginatively by means of sensitive juxtapositioning or original and inspired use of repetition.

The Dance Form

As soon as the first motif is composed, the imagined dance outcome becomes clearer in form. The composer begins to think of possible directions that it may take. For example, he/she may imagine:

a) an immediate repetition of the motif developed and varied, followed by an introduction of a new and contrasting motif, or

b) an introduction of another motif, as contrast to the first, followed by an interplay of the two.

According to experience, the composer, consciously or intuitively, employs the elements of form—repetition, variation, contrast, climax, proportion, balance, transition, logical development and unity. He/she may imagine some of these elements within the dance form before actually manipulating the material. He/she may, for example, consciously imagine the climax moments and work up to these through logical sequencing of the material content and placing of the dancers within the stage space.

It would seem, therefore, that the images construed within the composer's thought pose compositional problems and that these require further imaginative thought in order to solve them. This latter imaginative or original thought might produce even richer form than that imagined in the initial stages. The saying goes 'Let your imagination run away with you'. Often this occurs, and the composer may experience surprise with the results in composition. This element of surprise is as pertinent during the process of composition as it is in the viewing of it as a completed form:

A work of art always surprises us: it has worked its effect before we have become conscious of its presence.

Read (1931)

103

During composition, the composer's imagination is structured by the stimulus, by knowledge of movement material and, above all, by the 'technique peculiar to' dance construction. But within this framework there is freedom and the range and quality of the imagination used has a great deal to do with the ultimate success of the dance.

Intuition

> In building up his composition, the artist may proceed intellectually or instinctively, or perhaps more often partly by one method and partly by the other. But most of the great artists of the Renaissance—Piero della Francesca, Leonardo, Raphael—had a definite bias towards an intellectual construction, often based, like Greek sculpture or architecture, on a definite mathematical ratio. But when we come to Baroque composition like El Greco's 'Conversion of St. Maurice' the scheme is so intricate, so amazing in its repeated relations, so masterly in the reinforcement which gives form to intention, that the form itself, as often the solution of some mathematical problem, must have been an intuition.

Read (1931)

Although Read suggests that some great artists proceed either intellectually or instinctively, it is accepted by many that, in dance, the composer *must* allow intuition to guide him/her. At the same time he/she always needs to intellectualise because, during the process of composition, it is important to continually evaluate, select and memorise the movement content. The question is whether intuition is the main method of procedure, and how it is supported by knowledge which, for the dance composer, includes knowledge of movement as material and methods of constructing dance form.

Intuition Without Knowledge

The composer who relies mostly on intuition may produce something that is good and instinctively recognise it as such:

> It is recognised that the inspiration and conception of a work of art may often derive from the unconscious levels of the artist's personality and may not lie wholly open to deliberate, conscious apprehension. Hence the created work may embody fuller wealth of import than the artist

himself is aware of. Indeed it is sometimes maintained that the artist himself is not the best interpreter or exponent of his work.

Osborne (1968)

If the art work derives from the unconscious, without the support of knowledge, the form that emerges through intuition may only be successful once or even twice. Here the artist has hit upon something accidentally but, without knowledge of form, cannot begin to estimate why it is good and so never progresses beyond trial and error methods. In this situation, the composer experiences great frustration if he/she cannot be successful again and does not know why.

Knowledge Overruling Intuition

The composer who treats composition as an academic exercise often produces work which lacks feeling and warmth of human expression. The form may be sound theoretically but too predictable, and the content might lack the excitement that often derives from intuitive artistic flair.

Intuition with Knowledge

The middle line, of course, is the best route. The composer's natural feeling or artistry needs to be disciplined by knowledge and 'techniques peculiar to the art form'. For example, knowledge of principles of form guides the composer's intuitive inspiration whilst he/she is shaping the dance:

> These structural motives are very important in the making of a picture or any other plastic work of art, though they are not necessarily a deliberate choice of the artist.

Read (1931)

The more one works with principles the more they become a part of one's technique. The dance composer who has consciously manipulated the principles of form for long enough, will find that they become part of his/her sub-conscious. To some extent, the methods of constructing a dance will instinctively incorporate consideration of the elements of form. This is what Read may be implying when he says 'they are not necessarily a deliberate choice of the artist'. The artist's intuition is disciplined by the sub-conscious knowledge of form. But the intuition should be 'let loose' because the unique personal qualities which each work of art must possess can only emerge through the personal contribution of the artist and his/her intuitive feeling for art.

Intuition and Acquaintance Knowledge

The composer who performs or employs works of others will inevitably learn from them. If he/she has frequent opportunity to see dance in the theatre or study it as repertoire, he/she may gradually become perceptive of form, style and meaning and sub-consciously absorb a feeling for these elements which can be transposed into his/her own works. This learning can be acquired gradually through experience, but it is accelerated greatly if the composer has knowledge of form, style and meaning, per se. The student-composer who is in the process of learning about composition will be able to critically appraise what is seen within a clear frame of reference. The student without such knowledge appraises through feeling alone.

Experience of watching varied dance works and encountering works of other art forms, is perhaps a means of developing intuitive awareness and, even though it might not be a conscious awareness, the composer is bound to acquire an acquaintance knowledge of form which enhances his/her potential in dance composition.

Theoretical knowledge, supported by acquaintance knowledge of form, disciplines and guides the composer's intuition, but feeling must be allowed to penetrate and have an effect upon the work.

Knowing and Feeling

At best, the composer is knowledgable in terms of material for dance and methods of constructing a dance. He/she is also an experienced viewer of dances and has what is deemed a good imagination and a feeling for dance as art.

Knowledge of principles of composition and acquaintance knowledge of form, style and meaning in dance may be kept at a voluntary conscious level, or it might be so ingrained that it functions at the involuntary sub-conscious level. Imagination and intuition, inextricably interwoven with, and guided by, knowledge provide the bounds of the composer's freedom.

The inspirational moments always require intellectual evaluation and analysis so that they may properly fit into the form of the dance, but the rarity of the moments themselves are inex-

THE PROCESS OF COMPOSITION IN DANCE

COMPOSITION

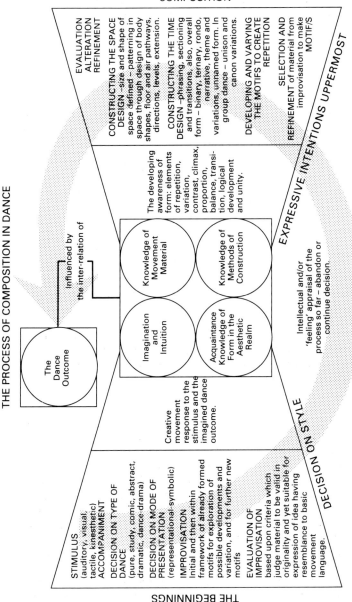

THE BEGINNINGS

EXPRESSIVE INTENTIONS UPPERMOST

DECISION ON STYLE

STIMULUS
(auditory, visual,
tactile, kinesthetic)
ACCOMPANIMENT

DECISION ON TYPE OF
DANCE
(pure, study, comic, abstract,
dramatic, dance-drama)

DECISION ON MODE OF
PRESENTATION
(representational-symbolic)

IMPROVISATION
Initial and then within
framework of already formed
motifs for exploration of
possible developments and
variation, and for further new
motifs

EVALUATION OF
IMPROVISATION
based upon criteria which
judge material to be valid in
originality and yet suitable for
expression of idea having
resemblance to basic
movement
language.

Creative
movement
response to the
stimulus and the
imagined dance
outcome.

The
Dance
Outcome

influenced by
the inter-relation of

Imagination
and
Intuition

Knowledge of
Movement
Material

Acquaintance
Knowledge of
Form in the
Aesthetic
Realm

Knowledge of
Methods of
Construction

Intellectual and/or
'feeling' appraisal of the
process so far – abandon or
continue decision.

The developing
awareness of
form: elements
of repetition,
variation,
contrast, climax,
proportion,
balance, transi-
tion, logical
development
and unity.

EVALUATION
ALTERATION
REFINEMENT

CONSTRUCTING THE SPACE
DESIGN –size and shape of
space defined – patterning in
space through design of body
shapes, floor and air pathways,
directions, levels, extension.

CONSTRUCTING THE TIME
DESIGN –phrasing, sectioning
and transitions; also, overall
form – binary, ternary, rondo,
narrative, theme and
variations, unnamed form. In
group dance – unison and
canon variations.

DEVELOPING AND VARYING
THE MOTIFS TO CREATE
REPETITION

SELECTION AND
REFINEMENT of material from
improvisation to make
MOTIF/S

plicable. The composer is constantly moving from feeling to knowing or the other way round. Somehow feeling and knowing merge on an indefinable plane. Discussion on this aspect of the compositional process can only go so far. However much is said, it remains but the 'tip of the iceberg'.

The important point here is that, whilst recognising the essential roles of imagination and intuition, it must also be clear that there exists a body of knowledge sufficient to guide and structure the movement outcomes of 'feeling and imagining' into order and form.

The table on page 107 may be taken to represent a summary of the discussion presented so far.

There is no distinct order of events during the process of composition. The curved arrow indicates a general direction, though there is bound to be a return to a particular stage at any time. For example, up until the last movement is selected the composer constantly needs to improvise and explore a range of possibilities.

EVALUATIONS

Response to a work of art is always based on prior experience which may grow to become discerning and mature. A dance can only be measured as successful in a relative sense. Relative to the onlooker's experience and background and the composer's stage of development in composing.

There is no objective formula for evaluation of a dance. It cannot be entirely processed by factual analysis, yet it is not merely judged on inner feelings or personal taste. Inevitably the onlooker will reflect intellectually about what is seen and, in viewing art, this is always influenced by aesthetic judgments:

> The word aesthetic comes from the Greek word, 'aesthesis' which means 'to perceive or to look at objects of interest'.
>
> Curl (1973)

Looking at something to appreciate and describe it aesthetically implies that we use:

> . . . concepts of shape, pattern, form, design; these then are the concepts appropriate to the aesthetic form of awareness, they connote perceptual characteristics.
>
> Curl (1973)

Most of us can appreciate an art work aesthetically but probably lack the ability to describe it. That which is aesthetically pleasing will *seem* right, significant, complete, balanced and unified, and we may *feel* these qualities rather than *know* them. Of course, each onlooker will perceive something different, but aesthetic evaluation will have much to do with the form of the dance. Some viewers might see the intricate shaping and changes of the designs of the dancers in relation to each other as being the most aesthetically pleasing aspect of the dance. Others might appreciate the quality of the dancers' movements, and the patterns into which these have been designed. A few may be pleased by the overall shape of the dance, and see the beginning, middle and end in proportionate relationship, and each section as a well balanced entity yet carefully blended into a unified whole. Others may feel a sense of pleasure on recognition of the repetitions and contrasts and follow the design of the dance within these frames of reference.

It could be that the emotional intensity of the dance completely immersed the viewer so that, after the experience, he/she remembered little of its form, only that it felt right at the time. Here, perhaps, the viewer has been less aesthetically and more dramatically moved with the dance. But one could say that the drama does not come across as significant unless embodied into a suitable shape, design or form.

It would appear, therefore, that aesthetic evaluation is to do with the onlooker's perception of the dance as a work of art having form, beauty and meaning. This is always accompanied with an inner and immeasurable appreciation of form in art which has grown for the viewer by virtue of experience in the total world of art, through pictures, poems, plays, films, sculptures, music as well as dance.

Intellectual reflection requires factual analysis which can occur only if there is knowledge. The critic might judge more objectively from this stand-point though there are no set criteria with which one dance can be judged against another. Each dance uses material and is constructed in a different way from every other dance, and this makes comparison in judgment a very difficult task. Nevertheless, intellectual reflection upon the following lines might be possible.

Consider the Whole Dance as a Work of Art

1. Has the composer reached the objective? Did the dance seem significant and worth watching, or was it obscure and meaningless?
2. Did the dance have continuity? Did it sustain interest throughout or were there some weak parts?
3. Was every part of the dance essential to the whole?
4. Was the style of the dance clearly established and then maintained throughout?
5. Was there enough depth and variety in the material content or was it too simple, naive and predictable?
6. Was the construction of the dance seen to have unity through its rhythmic structure?
7. Was there an element of surprise or was it all too easy to follow?
8. Was the choice of music—or other stimulus for accompaniment—suitable for the theme of the dance?
9. Was the dance constructed with an understanding of the stimulus?

After consideration of the dance as a whole art work, the

student of dance composition might persist further in intellectual reflection. There is more to a dance than its 'pieces' but these can be extracted and assessed. The following questions may help in this process.

1. **Consider the dance idea:**
   a) Was the basic idea behind the dance conveyed, only partly conveyed, or not conveyed at all?
   b) Were the movement images translatable?
   c) Did the form aid understanding of the underlying theme?
   d) Was the idea easily perceived or did the onlooker have to search intently to find meaning, and indeed, perhaps read into it that which was not meant to be?
   e) Was the topic too deep and involved for translation into dance movement?
   f) Simple ideas conveyed with artistry and originality often make the most successful dances. In pursuit of originality, however, has the composer chosen material which is too obscure in relation to the idea and, therefore, lost the simplicity by over-elaboration?
   g) Is it worth dancing about? Does it merit artistic expression? Does it have significance in the modern world?
   h) Does it cause emotional response and arouse the senses?
   i) Is the communication based on an individual distillation of expression or a hackneyed set of clichés?

2. **Consider the movement content:**
   a) Did the composer choose 'right' movements in relation to the idea?
   b) Was there a width of movement content which created variety and interest?
   c) Was there balance of action, qualitative, space and relationship emphasis or too much concentration on any one?
   d) Were the movements easily discernable as symbolic or representative of meaningful communication?

   ACTION
   e) Were the actions made interesting by varied co-ordinations and juxtapositioning?

111

f) Was the range of actions enough for the dance? (A range limited to nearly all gesture and positioning into body shape is a common fault.)

QUALITIES

g) Was there enough qualitative or dynamic variation in the dance?

h) Did the qualities colour the actions with appropriate light and shade enhancing the meaning?

SPACE

i) Was the spatial aspect of the movement relevant to the idea?

j) Did the composer utilise the stage space to best advantage and with consideration of locality and its expressive connotations?

k) Was the dance an interesting visual experience creating lines and shapes in space in harmony with the idea?

l) Was the use of focus a noticeable feature and did it communicate the intention?

m) Were the movements extended in space enough for the audience to appreciate them?

RELATIONSHIP

n) Were there enough dancers or too many for the idea?

o) Did the group relationship come over successfully?

p) Was the unison achieved?

q) Were the individuals placed advantageously in the group for the visual effect, or were some members masked by other dancers at any time?

r) Did the design of the group in terms of complementing body shapes, levels, and complementing movement patterns, emerge as successful and meaningful in the dance?

s) Did the solo stand out as important in the presence of the ground bass, or did it diminish by virtue of sheer strength of numbers in the preceding and following sections?

t) Was the number of dancers absolutely necessary at all times, or were there moments when the duos could have been solos and the trios could have been duos etc?

3. **Consider the construction elements of form:**
   a) Motif: Were the motifs apparent and foundational to the rest of the content of the dance?
   b) Repetition: Was there enough repetition to establish the meanings in the chosen movements or was repetition overstressed?
   c) Variety and Contrast: Did the dance utilise variety and contrast in the best and most appropriate ways, or was contrast just put in for its own sake without due reference to the total meaning?
   d) Climax or Highlights: How did the climaxes or highlights emerge? Were they apparent or forceful enough?
   e) Transition: Did the transitions merge into and become part of the whole and were they effectively employed as links between parts?
   f) Proportion and Balance: Was the dance balanced in terms of content or did one section appear irrelevant? Was one section too long and the other too short? Were they too much of the same length? Did the sections have interesting differences?
   g) Logical Development: Was the whole dance easy to follow? Did the idea emerge in a logical way, or were there many sudden changes in content confusing the issue? Did the end really emerge as important with a clear enough build-up, or was it left suspended?
   h) Unity: Did the whole become formed and a unified manifestation of the idea? Did the dance appear well constructed, each part having its role to play in forming a relevant, meaningful and artistic whole shape (which may be categorised as binary, or ternary or rondo etc.)?

4. **Consider the style:**
   a) Was the style selected suitable in expressing the theme?
   b) Was the dance coherent in style?
   c) Is the style relevant in today's dance context?
   d) In the event of the task requiring specific replication of a style, e.g. composed in Graham style or in Rock 'n' Roll style, is there sufficient understanding of and adherence to the details of the specified style.

e) If the task did not require specific replication of a known style, was there sufficient originality in use of the style or was it a direct copy of a known style without the composer's own 'signature'?

f) Were the performers able to present the style with sufficient clarity?

5. **Consider the performance:**
   a) Did the dancer's performance enrich or negate the dance composition?
   b) Was the performer sincere and involved in the rendering?
   c) Were the required technical skills mastered to the enhancement of the dance or did technical deficiency ruin the composition?
   d) Did the performer make real the images and movement content according to the composer's wishes or did personal interpretation alter the intention to some degree?
   e) Did the performers dance with a view to a communicative presentation to an audience or were they too involved within themselves, or the group, to make this positive?
   f) Was the style of the dance adhered to throughout its performance?

6. **Consider the stimulus as initiation of the dance:**
   a) Was the stimulus suitable for a dance to emerge from it?
   b) Was it apparent as an origin of the dance or did its relevance become lost?
   c) Was it viewed in a rich and artistically imaginative way to stimulate an interesting dance or was it translated too literally or too slightly?

7. **Consider the stimulus as accompaniment for dance:**
   a) If it (e.g. pole, cloak, material) was manipulated by the dancer/s was this done with ease and clarity or did it seem too difficult to manage?
   b) Did the accompanying object cause a lack of movement from the dancer/s?
   c) Was the accompanying stimulus too large or too much in itself rendering the dancer as minute and insignifi-

cant? (A film moving on the wall behind the dancers, for instance.)

d) If music was used as accompaniment:

i) Did it fit with the dance idea?

ii) Was it cut and abused for the purpose of the dance and therefore not valid or appropriate?

iii) Did the composer use the phrasing in the music or ignore it?

iv) Was the music too powerful or too slight for the dance? (A solo danced to an orchestral symphony, or a large dramatic group dance danced to a piano solo piece, for instance.)

v) Was the structure of the music in time suitably employed by the composer? (If a beat or 'pop' piece was used for instance, it would be unwise to move to every beat, on the other hand, if a piece is in strict $\frac{4}{4}$ time it would be inadvisable to swoop, swirl and move continuously through the beat.)

vi) Was the music really necessary and an inseparable part of the dance?

8. **Consider the other staging facets:**

a) Was the decor/lighting relevant to the idea?

b) Did the decor/lighting enhance the dance or overpower it?

c) Were the props placed correctly and did they have enough use to merit their presence?

d) Were the costumes relevant to the idea and the style of the dance?

e) Could the performers move easily without limitation in the costumes?

f) Was the make-up an enhancing feature?

g) Did any of the staging facets detract from the dance itself?

This list of questions, although extensive, is by no means exhaustive. Furthermore, it would be a cold and almost tortuous process to analyse and evaluate a dance by asking *all* these questions.

Inextricably bound with intellectual reflection on any level are the feelings of pleasure that an aesthetic work of art evokes in an onlooker. Each person experiences this pleasure in varying ways and in different degrees, but—in judging art—it is the fundamental criterion. Above all, therefore, the most important question to ask the viewer and the composer in relation to his/her own work, is whether or not the work was pleasing. *Did you like it?* If the answer is yes, there is, perhaps, no need for further evaluation, except that it can become a useful learning process to understand why it was appreciated. If the answer is no, then probably, reasons for its 'failure' can be found by asking *some* of the questions.

The teacher of dance composition would perhaps find the questions a useful frame of reference for constructively criticising a student's attempt in composition, but mentioning only the most salient points. Also, students of composition could, perhaps, criticise their own and other students' work by such questioning.

For the composer, such evaluations can only be made in retrospect and, probably, only after a period of time has elapsed since the completion of the dance. Personal satisfaction or dissatisfaction is the initial feeling of a composer, who may find that it is necessary to stand back from the actual experience in order to become more objective.

A last evaluation:

In the final analysis, a dance performance succeeds in generating enthusiasm when the audience is aesthetically stirred. It fails if an audience remains unmoved and unresponsive because feelings are left dormant.

An understanding of the 'rules' discovered through analytical essay and mastery of the craft of composition, helps towards the production of successful dances. When this understanding is combined with the composer's creative inspiration, born of imagination, intuition, artistry and vision, the dance will probably possess the elusive 'something' which assures successful impact.

CONCLUSION

This book has taken a close look at objectives, content, methods and evaluation in dance composition, and strongly suggests that theories, though necessary, are meant to be working statements.

As Dewey (1946) expressed it:

> They are not meant to be ideas frozen into absolute standards masquerading as eternal truth or programs rigidly adhered to; rather, theory is to serve as a guide in systematising knowledge . . .

Theory is practical in that it provides a guide for action. It clarifies and structures the processes of thought. Practice in adherence to a set of guidelines or principles will structure the process of thought that goes with the practical action of making a dance, but it is important to acknowledge that, in art, the guidelines are never fixed. There is no particular set which will predetermine a specific dance, or guarantee a successful outcome. It is certain, however, that the gifted composer, who may claim to work through insight only, has already assimilated the theory behind the practice.

The acquisition of concepts and their application in a discipline, such as the art of making dances, demands much time and diligent study. Learning is aided if the subject matter is structured from the simple to the complex. Experience of this kind can lead to the development of an ability to compose, but this demands a grasp of the interwoven nature of theory and practice. It is impossible to learn how to compose dances by reading alone, though by this means, much can be learned about the nature of form, aesthetics, style, communication and expression; all of which are vital aspects of the dance composer's growing knowledge.

The dance composer, constantly trying to relate theory and practice, faces a maze-like problem. At first, he/she needs clear signposts so that he/she may discover a way to the making of dances which have form and clarity. A consideration of the nature of these signposts and their regulating effect upon the work of the developing composer has been made in this book.

Section V

PRACTICAL ASSIGNMENTS
FOR STUDENTS

The following examples offer ideas for exploration in relation to the text in Sections I, II and III.

Progressively-staged instructions are given on separate pages. After each assignment, suggestions which may be helpful will be found.

Reference to a particular part of the text is given with each assignment but this only indicates an emphasis. The student-composer should constantly strive to integrate all aspects of the process of composition as far as he/she is able but, for study purposes, he/she may choose to make a dance stressing one facet. Indeed it is important that he/she attempts to solve different compositional problems each time a composition is made. In this way, the composer may gradually grow to understand the many contributory factors of expression and form which make dances works of art.

Many of these example assignments could be linked with a choice of stimulus. Some of the frameworks for composition might therefore be used several times with different stimuli. The student-composer should also endeavour to make dances of various styles – styles indigenous to countries, personal styles of choreographers, styles of different periods in history, and, of course, styles of different dance forms (e.g. contemporary, classical ballet, jazz, social).

IMPROVISATION

Action phrase: travel, turn, open, close, stretch.

Keep the sequence order but explore different ways of performing the actions. The exploration should stay within *action*.

Reference: Section I. Movement and Meaning.

---

1) Different ways to *travel:*
    a) using a variety of parts of the feet to take weight,
    b) leading with a variety of body parts into steps,
    c) step patterns (skips, hops, runs, gallops, slides, formed into repetitive sequences),
    d) on other body parts,
    e) on different body parts successively,
    f) emphasising bend, stretch or twist,
    g) adding jump and/or gestures and/or turns.

2) Different ways of *turning:*
    a) on both feet,
    b) from one foot to the other,
    c) on one foot,
    d) pivoting or spinning,
    e) jumping, hopping,
    f) inwards or outwards accompanied by arm and/or leg gestures,
    g) lead by different parts of the body,
    h) on different parts of the body,
    i) transferring weight during the turn onto different body parts.

3) Different ways of *opening, closing and stretching:*
    a) symmetrically or asymmetrically,
    b) with simultaneous or successive flow,
    c) parts of body isolated or whole body,
    d) lead by different body parts,
    e) near or far and various degrees within the range,
    f) with transference of weight or jumping.

IMPROVISATION

Action phrase: travel, turn, open, close, stretch.

Keep the sequence order but explore different ways of performing it emphasising *quality* variations.

Reference: Section I. Movement and Meaning.

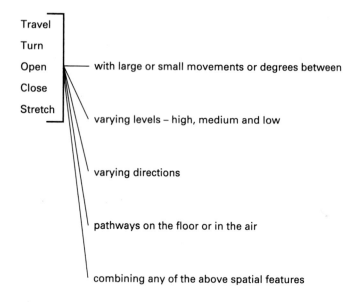

Travel
Turn
Open — with large or small movements or degrees between
Close
Stretch

varying levels – high, medium and low

varying directions

pathways on the floor or in the air

combining any of the above spatial features

IMPROVISATION

Action phrase: travel, turn, open, close, stretch.

Keep the sequence order but explore different ways of performing it emphasising *quality* variations.

Reference: Section I. Movement and Meaning.

Travel
Turn
Open
Close
Stretch

with time emphasis
– quickly or slowly
– accelerating or decelerating

with weight emphasis – strongly or lightly,
– increasing or decreasing degrees of tension

with flow emphasis
– bound stoppable and stopping or continuous and free

combining any of the above quality features

EXPLORATIONS IN MOVEMENT AND MEANING

Use each of the following phrases to express a different idea.
Try to find more than one idea for each phrase.

Action Phrases:

Phrase 1.
Rise . . .
Travel . . .
Close . . .
Fall . . .
Open . . .

Phrase 2.
Gesture leading into turn . . .
Travel into balance . . .
Tip into transference of weight . . .
Stretch and rise . . .
Travel and leap . . .

Phrase 3.
Leg gesture into stepping . . .
Open and turn . . .
Stand still . . .
Isolate and move three body parts in succession . . .
Curl . . .
Arm gesture into twist . . .

Reference: Section I. Movement and Meaning.

---

1) The student should attempt to define each idea by differentiation of the action content.

2) The accompanying qualitative content should alter within the phrase and be selected with a different emphasis for each of the ideas.

3) Each idea will also influence the way the space is used.

EXPLORATIONS IN MOVEMENT AND MEANING

Use each of the following phrases to express a different idea.
Try to find more than one idea for each phrase.

Quality Phrases:

Phrase 1.
From firm tension gradually lose tension to become light . . .
Move quickly and lightly. . .
Relax three parts of the body successively. . .
Become firm. . .
Release all tension and collapse. . .

Phrase 2.
Move with free flow. . .
Move with bound flow. . .
Make a series of bound and sudden movements. . .
Travel quickly, and with free flow to end in sudden and firm
stillness. . .

Phrase 3.
Move lightly and slowly. . .
Move slowly with changing tensions. . .
Move quickly alternating between firm and light qualities. . .
Spin accelerating and decelerating to end in a firm body
shape. . .

Reference: Section I. Movement and Meaning.

———————

The context of the expression must be adhered to throughout
the phrase. The quality changes should seem logical within the
chosen contexts. The mover's use of space and action should
enhance the expression and add interest to each phrase.

EXPLORATIONS IN MOVEMENT AND MEANING

Use each of the following phrases to express a different idea. Try to find more than one idea for each phrase.

Spatial Phrases:

Phrase 1.
Move with a constantly changing focus. . .
Move with a fixed focus. . .
Change focus and then move . . . repeat this three times. . .
Focus on one body part and move into different directions. . .
Focus high and then low. . .

Phrase 2.
Start with very small movements and increase in size to very large. . .
Move with very large movements. . .
Alternately move one side of the body with small gestures and the other side with large gestures. . .
Intersperse large and small movements. . .
Finish with one movement which gradually expands from a small shape to a large shape, or, the reverse. . .

Phrase 3.
Start in the centre of the dance area move backwards to centre back. . .
Move in a series of curves to end centre front. . .
Move slightly right and then left. . .
Move on a wide circular pathway to the right and end in the left back corner. . .
Move diagonally across the space from the left back corner to the right front corner. . .
Move backwards towards the centre and then exit from one of the four corners according to the expression. . .

Reference: Section I. Movement and Meaning.

———————

The context of the expression must be adhered to throughout the phrase. The spatial changes should seem relevant within the chosen contexts. The mover's use of action and quality should enhance the expression and add interest to the phrases.

EXPLORATIONS IN MOVEMENT AND MEANING

Relationship through group shapes and numerical variations:

1) For a group of three:
Start in a closed circle . . .
Become scattered and unrelated . . .
Dancer 1 move to dancer 2 . . .
Dancers 1 and 2 move to dancer 3 . . .
Move in a closed line . . .
Move to spread the line . . .
Make the line into a file and move . . .
Dancers 1 and 2 surround dancer 3 . . .
Make a circle . . .
Become very close and in contact with each other . . .
Select an appropriate ending . . .

Decide on a dance idea suitable for this framework and select movement content for composition.

2) For a group of four:
Create a framework as above stressing symmetry in group shape and numerical arrangement.
Decide on a dance idea suitable for this framework and select movement content for composition.

3) For a group of seven:
Create a framework stressing asymmetry in group shape and numerical arrangement.
Decide on a dance idea suitable for this framework and select movement content for composition.

Reference: Methods of Construction III.

---

1) The dance idea will define the action, quality and spatial content which should be compatible with the set group shapes and numerical relationships.

2) The created frameworks should contain a variety of group shapes and numerical arrangements. Too much variety, however, would lead to confused and unconnected happenings.

3) Each group shape and numerical arrangement can be retained for varying lengths of time in the dance. (One may be

kept for several phrases of movement and another could be used only transitorily.)

4) As additional challenge for advanced students, consideration of the use of the stage space in relation to a specified 'front' might be included.

EXPLORATIONS IN MOVEMENT AND MEANING

Relationship through ground pattern and numerical arrangements for six or more dancers:

1) On paper, make a series of diagrams which show ground patterns and numerical arrangements inviting a variety of relationships.

2) Select a dance idea which suits the use of this spatial and relationship framework.

3) Compose a dance selecting appropriate movement content and using the set ground patterns and numerical arrangements.

Reference: Methods of Construction III.

---

1) The ground pattern should use all the space available and consist of a mixture of design, such as curves, straight lines and angles. The dancers should be numerically divided in many ways and the spatial positioning of each dancer should be clearly shown on the ground pattern diagrams.

2) The dance idea will define the action and quality content. While the floor patterning and numerical relationship is set, the other aspects of spatial design (group shape, levels, directions, focus) and relationships (face to face, back to back, in contact, surrounding) can be selected to fit the idea.

3) The idea and the set framework should be compatible and merge into a meaningful dance form.

IMPROVISATION

Hover
Twist
Swirl
Skim
Lift
Dip
Fall   Explore some of these words as stimuli.
Circle   Improvise and then compose motifs to depict
Sway   one of the following ideas:

Movement of the Wind.   A Fairground.
Movement of the Sea.   Lost.
Movement of Birds.   Insanity.

Reference: Section I. Material Content.

The action words have rhythmic characteristics and, therefore, have an implied quality content.

Linking them in different orders will vary phrase rhythms and each idea will suggest certain patterns of juxtapositioning.

Further differentiation can be achieved through the spatial patterning (placing, direction, level, size, pathways) of the movements.

Before selecting material for the motifs, the solo dancer might improvise for some time changing the order of the word stimuli.

Further exploration in twos or groups might extend the range of interpretation implicit in the words.

COMPOSITION

Motif and Development.

1) Use a simple action motif such as:
    a) side and close,
  or b) sway right and left,
  or c) four walks,
  or d) a waltz step,
and develop it in *action* increasing the complexity until it is as full as possible involving a multiplicity of body parts.

2) Make a study showing the simple beginning, an increase in complexity, a decrease in complexity and a return to the beginning motif.

Reference: Methods of Construction II.

---

1) The following developments might be incorporated:
    a) taking weight on various parts of the feet,
    b) leading with various parts of the feet or other body parts,
    c) emphasising bend, stretch and/or twist,
    d) adding arm and/or leg gestures, also gestures of other body parts,
    e) transferring weight onto other body parts,
    f) adding jumps,
    g) adding turns,
    h) emphasising travel,
    i) changing body shapes.

2) The climax of a steady build-up in complexity should show a richness of action content within the motif itself, whereas the build-up or reducing phases of the study might contain developments on parts of the motif maintaining the rest as it was originally. The climax should have developments throughout the whole of the motif.

COMPOSITION

Motif and Development.

1) Use a simple action motif such as:
    a) side and close step,
  or b) gesture, step, waltz step,
  or c) gesture, turn, sway right and left,
  or d) two steps into leg and arm gesture,
and develop it *qualitatively* increasing the complexity until it is as full as possible.

2) Make a study showing a simple beginning, an increase in complexity, a decrease in complexity and a return to the beginning motif.

Reference: Methods of Construction II.

---

1) The following developments might be incorporated:
    a) emphasis on one factor (time, weight or flow), changing with each repetition of the whole motif, or changing during the motif,
    b) emphasis on two factors changing with each repetition of the whole motif or changing during the motif,
    c) emphasis on three factors (time, weight, flow), changing with each repetition of the whole motif, or changing during the motif.

2) The motif should be given qualitative identity to start with and then developments can be seen as changes while the action remains the same.

COMPOSITION

Motif and Development.

1) Use a simple action motif such as:
      a) side and close step with arm gesture
  then b) sway right and left   "   "   "
  then c) four walks   "   "   "
  then d) waltz steps   "   "   "
and develop it *spatially* increasing the complexity until it is full in spatial terms.

2) Make a short solo study showing the simple beginning, an increase in complexity, a decrease in complexity and a return to the beginning motif.

Reference: Methods of Construction II.

---

1) The following developments might be incorporated:
  a) varying the size and/or level of actions,
  b) varying the directions of the steps of the whole motif or parts of the motif—also stressing different directions in other body parts,
  c) taking the action on different pathways—curves or straight lines—to make a variety of floor patterns.

2) The motif should have a spatial identity to start with, for instance, side and close and sway right and left stresses the side direction; although the arm gesture may take a different direction, the walks naturally take a forward direction and the waltz step contains rise and fall or up and down movement. These spatial aspects can be changed while the action remains identifiable throughout.

COMPOSITION

1) Go through the possible developments and variations of the action of a side and close step as detailed in Methods of Construction II.

2) In twos: structure a short dance based upon this motif with
either   a court-like style
or   a comic flavour

Reference: Methods of Construction II.

The characteristics given to the starting side and close must be retained for long enough and then followed logically by another way of performing side and close. Use about four or five ways only with developments on these.

The duo relationship should be varied and interesting.

COMPOSITION

Motif, development and variation for a solo.

1) a) Compose a phrase motif to approximately 16 bars of music.
   b) Repeat it exactly but emphasising the other side of the body.
   c) Develop and vary it spatially.
   d) Develop and vary its quality content.
   e) Develop and vary its action content by simultaneously combining more actions with the original actions.
   f) Develop and vary the phrase so that the space, quality and action content are slightly altered throughout.
   g) Extract a small part of the motif and repeat it in four different ways.
   h) Repeat the original phrase in a different order.

2) Select 4 or 5 of the above phrases and link them to compose a study form.

Reference: Methods of Construction II.

The phrases could be linked so that the developments occur end on or simultaneously. The study should be a whole shape, each part leading naturally to the next.

COMPOSITION

1) Improvise with literal movement to show one of the following moods:
   a) boredom
   b) carefree and frivolous
   c) frustrated anger.

2) Select several movements and transform them into symbolic movements.

3) Make a phrase motif linking the movements into a logical order.

4) Repeat the motif with developments.

Reference: Methods of Construction I and II.

---

1) The improvisation should be within a range of movement normally associated with the 'everyday' expression of the moods.

2) The actions might then be transformed by enlargement, (increase in size — the movement involving more of the body — extending further in space) performing it with a different body part/s, emphasising or altering its rhythmic structure, adding more action (e.g. jumps added to the shaking fist action for anger). All this results in development and variation of the original representative movement. The degree of development or variation will determine the movement as 'mostly representative' or 'mostly symbolic'.

3) The repetition should extend even further towards symbolic presentation.

COMPOSITION

1) a) Start with four walks forward.
   b) Change the rhythm.
   c) Retain b) and add a leg gesture to one of the walks.
   d) Retain b) & c) and add an arm gesture to one of the walks.
   e) Retain b) c) & d) and add a turn to one of the walks.
   f) Retain b) c) d) & e) and add a jump to one of the walks.
   g) Retain b) c) d) e) & f) and add low level to one of the walks.
   h) Retain b) c) d) e) f) & g) and add weight on different parts of the feet where appropriate.

2) Take the final outcome (a rich four walk action motif) and use it as a basis for a dance—disintegrating it, extracting from it, altering its order, developing and varying its content.

Reference: Methods of Construction II.

———————————

Once the motif has been made it should be put to one side.

The composer is advised to select a small part as a starting point and then allow the dance to grow logically.

The overall original motif may never be used in the completed dance but its pieces will provide a relationship of content throughout.

The dance could be further stimulated by an idea which might have occurred to the composer during the exploration of the four walks.

COMPOSITION

1) Make a floor pattern motif using straight lines.

2) Make a floor pattern motif using curved pathways.

3) Create step patterns which are suitable for the floor patterns and employ legato or sustained and staccato or sudden qualities to emphasise the angularity or curvature.

4) Compose a short solo study establishing the material as follows:
   a) floor pattern using straight lines,
   b) floor pattern using curved lines,
   c) floor patterns with step patterns including defined qualities,
   d) developments and variations of c) amalgamating parts of the two patterns.

Reference: Methods of Construction II.

The study will become more complex in action and quality terms but the floor patterns should emerge as a constant and most important feature. They will appear more complex when parts of each are amalgamated.

COMPOSITION

Motif, development and variation for a duo:

1) Compose a *solo* phrase motif.

2) Use the phrase motif for two dancers—in unison using the same or complementary movements.

3) Repeat the phrase developing and varying the content and at some time employ canon using the same and complementary movements.

Reference: Methods of Construction III.

———————————

1) If this assignment is given to two student-composers, both should learn and be able to dance the solo motif. This is then adapted for composition of a duo, and the first phrase introduces the motif as material for two dancers.

2) The original motif should be performed by one or other of the dancers throughout this first phrase. In complementing, the student will naturally develop the original content. The development will be seen *at the same time* as the original.

3) The developments or variations of the original can be performed by both dancers in unison or canon.

COMPOSITION

Motif and development for a *group* (4–7)

1) Compose a solo motif lasting about 16 bars of music. Establish the motif for the group in unison.

2) Compose several repetitions of parts or the whole of the motif emphasising variation within time (as illustrated on page 58) and include as many numerical divisions and spatial differentiations as possible.

Reference: Methods of Construction II and III.

---

1) The motif can be split into parts, changed in order of its parts developed and varied by any means (action, quality, space or only by relationship).

2) The spatial and relationship design should enhance the presentation.

3) The orchestration in time should emerge as the prominent feature.

4) It will probably be found that the process requires a director 'out in front'.

5) There should not be too much going on at one time.

COMPOSITION

For three dancers:

1) Work individually and make a phrase motif for one of the following characters:

> slow, gentle day-dreamer
> quick, lively, exuberant
> strong, forceful, dominating

2) Make a dance which successively brings each character to the foreground. Each character should perform his/her own phrase motif while the other two, through unison or canon background, copy, complement or contrast the motif but retain their individual characteristics.

Reference: Methods of Construction III.

---

1) The three motifs should be contrasting in use of action, qualities and space.

2) The relationship of the three in terms of placing, focus and level should be interesting (the use of rostra could enhance the presentation).

3) While one character is performing the motif, the other two could complement, copy or contrast it, by doing the same movement but with different qualitative emphasis or, by developing and varying the movement (e.g. a slow gentle turn at medium level taken by the dreamy character could be accompanied by a fast double turn at high level performed by the quick, lively character and a firm travelling action on a circular pathway performed by the dominator) or, contrasting the movement with one from their own motifs. (This contrast should not occur too often since it is difficult to view, though intermittent previews or reviews of parts of motifs might be interesting.)

COMPOSITION

Solo or group.

1) Find a song or poem with a chorus and verse arrangement.

2) Make a motif for the chorus interpreting the mood and/or meaning of the words.

3) Make motifs for the verses trying to keep a sense of the changing meaning and yet retaining a movement relationship from verse to verse.

4) Make a dance in rondo form developing and varying the chorus' movement content each time in slightly different ways, taking care that they can follow and lead into each new verse.

Reference: Methods of Construction II, III and IV.

---

1) The song or poem should be suitable for interpretation into dance.

2) The essence of meaning should emerge through the movement—some of the words might be clearly interpreted and others not at all. The accompaniment and dance should merge successfully—neither of them dominating the other.

3) The style or manner in which the movements in each chorus are performed should be adhered to throughout. The composer has the task of identifying the aspects of movement he/she wishes to retain in the verses to relate each one to the others. For instance, he/she may keep a 'swing' quality and use different actions and spatial patterns to keep to the context of the words.

4) The choruses should retain enough of the original to be clearly identified.

COMPOSITION

Solo study:

1) Make two contrasting motifs.

2) Present the whole as A, B, then an amalgamation of A and B retaining the original content exactly, as far as possible.

3) Repeat an amalgam of A and B but with development and variation.

Reference: Methods of Construction IV—binary form.

———————————

1) The A and B motifs should be distinctive from each other.

2) In the first amalgamation it will be difficult to achieve logical development. The movements within each motif can be taken out of order. Some may not fit at all and, therefore, are best left out.

3) The second amalgamation could follow the order of the first but contain development and variation of the content.

COMPOSITION

Transition:

Given two short sequences of movement which are contrasted
—make two different transitions to link them.

Reference: Methods of Construction V.

Each transition should contain a flavour of both sequences.

One of them may be mostly repetitive of the first, intermittently introducing the second sequence. The other may retain
only one aspect of the first, for instance, the quality content
while introducing the action and spatial content of the second.

RESOURCE BASED LEARNING INTO COMPOSITION

Style:

Using video, study a section of choreograpy which you would call 'mainstream' contemporary dance and note which of the following stylistic features are evident:

feet in parallel and all parts of the feet used sensitively
trunk/centre of body important in all movements
weight shifts into and out of balances
contractions and release with upward focus
tipping into and out of movements to achieve an ongoing feel
hips initiating moves or extending beyond the centre line
floorwork—moves into, across, on and out of floor
natural opposition of arms and legs as in walking
emphasis on qualities of swing, impulse and impact
variety in length of phrases and rhythmic patterning

Select at least four of the above stylistic features and create a short solo study (2 minutes in duration) to perform to a colleague having given him/her the list first. Your colleague should then determine which four factors you emphasised and how you might improve your performance of them.

Reference: Methods of Construction VI.

The section of choreography on video should be short and permit the student to use slow motion, freeze frame and repetition of phrases.

The style in the student's own composition should be clearly defined and coherent.

RESOURCE BASED LEARNING INTO COMPOSITION

Style:

Using video, select a section of choreography that you would label 'jazz' in style, e.g. Robert North's 'Lonely Town, Lonely Street' (1984). Study it and note which of the following stylistic features are present:

movements initiated and isolated to specific body parts e.g. hips, shoulders
accented beats and syncopated rhythms
downward stressed grounded movements
sharp changes of direction and focus
quick, short steps interspersed with long, smooth steps
strong, sharp (percussive) contractions of centre of body and other body parts e.g. elbows
use of still held positions
emphasis on use of knees to give different qualities
emphasis of medium level in space

1) Copy the first phrase of the section and then add another phrase of your own to it retaining the stylistic features you noted from above.

2) Contrast these phrases with another phrase emphasising stylistic features which were not evident in the video section.

3) Link the two pieces of composition into A and B motifs and create a group dance for five based on them.

Reference: Methods of Construction VI.

———————————

1) The section of choreography on video should be a short solo and facilities for slow motion, freeze frame and repetition of it should be available to the students. They will probably need help in 'turning it around' i.e. copying the movements of a front facing dancer on the screen.

2) To fulfil this task students should have a suitable vocabulary of jazz movements. (A book such as 'Modern Jazz Dance' by Dolores Kirton Cayou could be a helpful additional source here.)

3) The group dance should employ time and space design features (Methods of Construction III) and retain a coherence of jazz style.

RESOURCE BASED LEARNING INTO COMPOSITION

Style

Find a theme for a dance which requires you to distil the essence of an ethnic dance style and combine it with a Western contemporary or classical ballet style.

1) Research the ethnic dance style noting its distinctive characteristics i.e. kinds of actions, qualities, spatial and relationship features.

2) View and study dance works of professional choreographers who have used an ethnic dance style in this way—e.g. Christopher Bruce's 'Sergeant Early's Dream' (1986), 'Ghost Dances' (1981), 'Cruel Garden' (1977) and Jiri Kylian's 'Stamping Ground' (1982).

3) Work out ways in which you can combine the two dance styles to make an original combination of them and at the same time convey your idea.

Reference: Methods of Construction VI.

———————————

1) The research should, as far as it is possible, involve the student in studying the ethnic dance style at source e.g. a particular form of African dance, S. Asian (e.g. Bharatha Natyam), Aboriginal, Chinese. Study should include consideration of cultural influences on the dance style.

2) The viewing of dance works should be guided so that students can determine which characteristics derive from the ethnic form and which are Western in origin.

3) The student's work should show evidence of three styles merging—the ethnic, the Western and his or her own style.

APPRECIATION INTO COMPOSITION AND PERFORMANCE

Resource-based teaching/learning.

Resource: Intimate Pages (1984) Choreographed by Christopher Bruce

Activity A: Small group discussion—no more than five.

Video snippet—the beginning phrases up until the woman has stroked the man's head with her right hand. This should be available in isolation from the rest of the dance work and as an easily repeatable video resource.

1) Can you find two phrases and the beginning of a third phrase? What starts and ends each phrase?

2) What sort of feelings are the man and woman expressing?

Write down your answers to present to others.

Activity B: Study of choreography and practical composition task in twos.

Video snippet—same as above viewed several times as required.

1) Describe and list the spatial relationships between the dancers (e.g. facing, at side of, on) in:
   a) phrase 1 and,   b) phrase 2
Is there a difference in the relationships shown in the two phrases?

2) Describe the changes of speed you see. Why do you think the choreographer uses these?

3) Duo task—practical composition:

Choose one of the following ideas:

   an argument—forbidden love—despondence

Discuss the meanings you wish to convey. Use at least three of the duo relationships you listed in 1) above as a basis for a short dance sequence.

Activity C: Refining the composition and practising performance of it.

Video snippet—as above—view as many times as required.

1) Watch how the dancers link their movements to make the
phrases fluid and continuous.

   — Watch also for the pauses.

   Make your own composition clear in its use of continuity
   and pauses and then practise it paying particular attention to continuity and pauses in conveying the meanings.

2) Watch the video again.

   — Are the pauses dead still? If not, what keeps the dance
   movement going at these points?
   — Practise your duo again working on the pauses to make
   them 'live and breathe'.

3) Have your duo videoed and then discuss with your partner
ways in which your performance could be improved.

   — Write a self-assessment on the composition and on your
   own performance in the duo.

See expectations of learning related to these tasks in Section
III. Resource-based Teaching/Learning of Dance Composition.

APPRECIATION OF DANCE—A THEATRE VISIT

Before going to see the performance

Before going to a performance answer the following questions and do the following tasks. They have been designed to help you notice things about the performance you are going to see. Please note that there are no right or wrong answers and that more than one word could be listed in those questions that ask you to do this.

1) There are some words or concepts that can help us understand better the type of dance we are wtaching. Certain words seem to describe certain situations. *Comic and dramatic* are easy to use. A *dance-drama* tells a story. *Pure dance* would have nothing to do with anything except the dance movements themselves. Some people call this *abstract* dance but abstract dance might also be based on the movement of birds or the colours in a spectrum, for example, or anything 'abstracted' from something else. (See Methods of Construction I.)

From the following labels, try to select that which suitably describes the situations below: *dramatic dance, dance-drama, abstract dance, comic dance, pure dance.*

Remember there are no right or wrong answers and that for some situations more than one label might be appropriate.

a) A dance work depicting the event of an earthquake.
b) A dance work with a movement theme of curves, circles and spirals.
c) A dance work which depicts the movement of the sea.
d) A dance work which is titled 'Concerto' and is inspired by music alone.
e) A dance work using a nonsense rhyme.
f) A dance work called 'Magnetism' which uses electronic music.

2) Dance movements always communicate something, i.e. ideas, feelings, events, characteristics. When we see dances and want to talk about them we need words to describe the expression in the movements.

Look at picture 16 on page 62. List any of the following words which seem to describe the expression in the movement.

147

Exhilaration, powerfulness, playfulness, energy, freedom, joy, strength.

3) We need words also to describe the particular qualities we can see in a movement.

Which of the following words would you use to describe the qualities in the movement:

buoyant, tense, graceful, strong, curved, flowing, delicate, angular.

4) Often it is the shape or line created in the space that makes us notice a movement.

Look at picture 11 on page 60.

a) Can you find curves, straight lines, and angles created by the pair?
b) What shape are the spaces created by the dancers' limbs?
c) What shape in space does the duo create?

5) Now that we have some words, we can use them and others to describe dance movements.

In the following examples the choreographer is trying to express feelings.

a) Imagine a dance which expresses gaiety, joyfulness and exhilaration. What sort of movements would the choreographer use to express this mood?
b) Think of another feeling, describe it and the sort of movements you might expect in a dance which depicts it.

6) When we talk about dance works we need to refer to other aspects besides the movement, i.e. the sound accompaniment, the design of the set, the lighting, the props, the make-up and costumes.

a) In a small group discuss the role of each of these aspects in a dance work that you have seen recently.
b) Write notes on each aspect and how it contributed to the expression/meaning in the dance.

Now see the performance. Enjoy it and trust your own feelings about it.

After the performance

After the performance answer the following questions and do the following tasks in relation to the dance work you saw. (If there was more than one work choose the one you liked best.)

1) Your programme can give you a lot of information. Use it to answer the following.

a) What dance work did you see?
b) Who choreographed it and when was it first produced?
c) Name the designer and briefly describe the set, the lighting, and the costumes.
d) Who composed the music and what sort was it (e.g. electronic, jazz, vocal sound, classical, etc.)?

2) You will soon be writing a review of the dance work. To help you, let's first make some more observations.

a) What type of dance work was it (dance-drama, pure dance, abstract, etc.)? Perhaps it was a combination of two or more types.
   b) What was the style of the work (e.g. classical, jazz, folk, modern, etc.)?
c) Name two of the dancers and write a few sentences about their performances.

3) The meaning of the dance work is not something that is predetermined, but is entirely up to you, the member of the audience. Of course, the dance may not be 'about' anything at all.

a) What do you think were the main ideas or feelings expressed in the dance work by the choreographer?
b) How did it make *you* feel?
c) Try to remember which movements you think most expressed the ideas or feelings contained in the dance. Describe two of these movements and say why you think they most expressed the ideas or feelings.

4) Closely observing the dance work takes practice.

a) List any of the following that you noticed about the dance. You can add your own observations to those below.

An important pattern of movement was repeated several times.

Movement in unison was used.

Sometimes the dancers did the same movements one after the other.

There was a lot of variety in the movement content of the dance work.

The patterns and shapes the dancers made were interesting and varied.

All the various parts or sections of the dance seemed to fit together well.

b) Can you make a list of words to describe qualities of movements in the dance work? If you consider the work to consist of different sections, how do the words for one section compare with those for another?

c) Visualize a particularly exciting or memorable moment from the dance. Can you make a drawing of it?

5) You are now quite ready to write a review of the dance work. Look through your work from before the performance and afterwards and make sure that in your review you consider all the aspects i.e. choreography, set design, lighting, costumes, etc.

Informed, opinionated members of the public are just as important to dance as dancers.

PRESENTATION OF DANCE TO AN AUDIENCE

Alignment: observing and structuring movement into advantageous alignment.

1) Presented with a phrase of continuous movement emphasising pattern in space, the student-composer should observe it and:
   a) correct the alignment of the body in relation to the front during any of the movements which are lost to the audience, and
   b) find about 4–6 stopping places within the phrase which shows pleasing alignment in relation to an audience.

2) Have the dancer repeat the continuous movement phrase until the corrections in a) above have been mastered.

3) Have the dancer repeat the phrase with the agreed stops and make sure that an audience could appreciate the spatial patterns in movement and the body shapes in stillness. Define also, the nature of the stillnesses, whether breath moments which seem to continue in movement often through line, or, absolute and held stillness. The latter require perfect alignment.

Reference: Methods of Construction II.

————————————

There is no set criterion for good alignment but the following guidelines might be helpful:

   a) avoid using the forward and backward directions in gestures when facing the front or back. These lines are better placed sideways or diagonally in relation to an audience.
   b) Try to get the performer to *feel* a sense of line throughout the body, e.g. an open diagonal line from high-right to deep-left requires a tilt from the waist so that the line passes through and beyond the shoulders in a straight line.
   c) The positioning of body parts to give the maximum effect to body shape needs to be carefully analysed in an aesthetic way. Just as in a photograph, a small tilt of the head could make all the difference to the total body shape and its meaning.

151

d) If the moments of stillness are required to 'live on', try to get the performer to achieve a sense of movement through and beyond the lines and curves the body is making. Then the audience may momentarily visually extend these lines or curves from the dancer's extremities on into space.

PRESENTATION OF DANCE TO AN AUDIENCE

Observation of relationship.

1) Two observers watch eight dancers. Each dancer should compose a short sequence using a spatial form based on a picture.

2) Each of the observers should select two dancers whose sequences seem to complement each other.

3) Keep the sequences as composed but by means of spatial placing, timing and pausing, create an illusion of duo relationship.

Reference: Methods of Construction III.

---

1) The observer could look for some of the following features:
   a) repetition of design in the two bodies,
   b) repetition of air pathways,
   c) repetition in direction,
   d) complementing action,
   e) contrast in levels.

2) When the duo relationship is made it might appear harmonious and related like a two-part song.

3) The observer should work from one front and concentrate upon the visual design created by the two bodies.

PRESENTATION OF DANCE TO AN AUDIENCE

Observation of relationship:

1) Select *one* of the following ideas:
   a) Peace and Sympathy
   b) Streetwise — Gamins
   c) Workers
   d) Growing Excitement
   e) Or any other scene-setting situation (perhaps an opening to a dance-drama)

2) Have six couples compose short duo sequences.

3) The composer/observer could then manipulate the six couple sequences, by means of spatial placing, timing and pausing, into a group of related couples. He/she could look for matching and complementary movement and use these parts of the sequences simultaneously. He/she should aim to use stillness at different times for each couple and avoid having more than three couples moving at the same time unless the movements are the same or very complementary.

4) Since each couple will be doing something different the above structure of their relationship should aim for unity. To reinforce the unity, it might then be appropriate to create a transition to be performed in unison before the group dance ends or goes on to another section.

It is essential that the composer/observer works from the front. He/she can then aim to focus the attention on the various moving parts of the group in interesting ways. For instance, this could be effected by having a couple towards the centre-back start, and then a front corner couple complement their action a moment later. There are endless ways of initiating, interrupting and linking moments of each of the couples' sequences and the composer should constantly stand back to evaluate the effect.

COMPOSITION AND EVALUATION

With a group of 7:

1) Discover appropriate numerical variations, group shapes and spatial (as if in photographs) placings to express one of the following:
   a) Children's Games
   b) Villagers Mourning War Victims
   c) Dictators and Oppressed
   d) Cardboard City

2) Form a dance using some of the discovered group shapes and spatial placings.

3) After completion attempt to evaluate the dance in terms of the principles of balance and proportion.

Reference: Methods of Construction III and V.

Numerical relationship should be varied as much as possible. The area defined for the dance should be used to the fullest extent, with the groups placed in a variety of places within the area and in different relationship with each other. The use of props or rostra could enhance the presentation.

COMPOSITION AND EVALUATION

1) Compose a dance.

2) Report in writing on the emergence of the idea/motivation and why the stimulus was chosen. Describe the form of the composition and give details of the material content with reasons for its choice.

Reference: Section II.

———————————

COMPOSITION PROBLEMS

Assignments for more advanced students suitable for exploration, written report and group discussion:

1) a) Make an action phrase.
   b) Manipulate it to make it comic in two different ways.
   c) Demonstrate and explain how this has been achieved.
   d) Find general principles which arise out of the work.

2) a) Make a phrase of movement for two people which shows them to be very dramatically involved with each other.
   b) Discover ways of keeping this involvement yet projecting it to the audience.
   c) Detail possible answers to the problem of projection of dramatic involvement.

3) a) With a group of six find and demonstrate as many numerical relationships, placement relationships and group shapes as possible.
   b) Present views on the expressive connotations implicit in them.

4) a) Make simple dance phrases to express i) sorrow ii) excitement.
   b) Make both the phrases dramatic.
   c) Explain how the movement was dramatised.

5) a) Find several representational movements which suggest: i) an old aged character   ii) a group of gossips.
   b) Make two phrases of symbolic movement utilising the above.
   c) Explain how representation of the characters was retained without the use of mime.

6) a) Make two simple dance phrases based on a non-European dance style (e.g. South Asian, Afro-Caribbean) – abstracting the essence of the style.
   b) Use the two phrases as motifs for a dance based upon a story or custom of the place of origin.
   c) Explain how the motifs were adapted/extended to tell the story and how the style was defined.

References

Best D. (1985) *Feeling and Reason in the Arts*. Allen and Unwin.

Curl G. (1973) Lecture on Aesthetic Judgments in Dance in *Collected Conference Papers in Dance*—A.T.C.D.E.

Dewey J. (1946) *The Public and its Problems*. Gateway Books.

Hayes E.R. (1955) *Dance Composition and Production for High Schools and Colleges*. The Ronald Press.

H'Doubler M.N. (1957) *Dance: A Creative Art Experience*. University of Wisconsin Press.

Jowitt D. (1988) *Time and the Dancing Image*. University of California Press.

Laban R. (1948) *Modern Educational Dance*. Macdonald & Evans.

Laban, R. (1960) *The Mastery of Movement*, second edition revised by L. Ullmann. Macdonald & Evans.

Langer S. (1953) *Feeling and Form*. Routledge & Kegan Paul.

Martin J. (1933) *The Modern Dance*. Dance Horizons Inc.

Osborne H. (1968) *Aesthetics and Art Theory. An Historical Introduction*. Longmans, Green.

Preston-Dunlop V. (1963) *A Handbook for Modern Educational Dance*. Macdonald & Evans.

Read H. (1931) *The Meaning of Art*. Penguin.

Redfern H.B. (1973) *Concepts in Modern Educational Dance*. Henry Kimpton.

Reid A.L. (1969) Lecture on Aesthetics and Education. Conference Report Association of Principals of Women's Colleges of Physical Education.

Seigel M. (1979) *The Shapes of Change*. Avon Books.

Smith J.M. (1983) Technique and Style as Aspects of Expression in Dance in *Collected Conference Papers in Dance Volume* **3** NATFHE.

Smith J.M. and Newman S. (1978) *Dance Appreciation Teaching Units for Schools and Colleges*. Ballet Rambert and Thames Polytechnic.

Video sources:

Bruce C. (1984) *Intimate Pages* and (1986) *Sergeant Early's Dream* on *An Evening with the Ballet Rambert Company* Virgin Classics, VVD 346 VHS (1986).

Kylian J. (1984) *L'Enfant et les Sortilèges* Netherlands Dans Theater, produced by Virgin Video VVD 382 (1986).

North, R. (1984) *Lonely Town, Lonely Street* on *An Evening with the Ballet Rambert Company* Virgin Classics, VVD 346 VHS (1986).

Further reading

Adshead J. (1981) *The Study of Dance*. Dance Books Ltd.

Adshead J (ed.) (1986) *Choreography—Principles & Practice*. Study of Dance Conference 4 NRCD University of Surrey.

Allcock R. and Bland V. (1980) *Dance in Education*. Dance Books Ltd.

Beatty P. (1989) *Form without Formula a concise guide to the choreographic process*. Press of Terpsichore Ltd.

Cheney G. (1989) *Basic Concepts in Modern Dance*. A Dance Horizons Book, Princeton Book Co.

Cohan R. (1986) *The Dance Workshop*. Unwin Paperbacks.

Haynes A. (1987) Changing Perspectives in Dance Education in Abbs P. (ed.) *Living Powers*, The Falmer Press.

Kirton Cayou D. (1976) *Modern Jazz Dance*. Unwin Brothers Ltd.

Lowden M. (1989) *Dancing to Learn*. The Falmer Press.

Reid L.A. (1983) Aesthetic Knowing in Ross M. *The Arts a Way of Knowing*. Pergamon Press.

Redfern H.B. (1983) *Dance, Art and Aesthetics*. Dance Books Ltd.

Redfern H.B. (1986) *Questions in Aesthetic Education*. Allen and Unwin.

Robertson A. and Hutera D. (1988) *The Dance Handbook*. Longman Group UK.

Smith J.M. (1988) *Dance as Art Education: New Directions in Young People Dancing 4th International Conference*. Dance and the Child International—Volume 1—Dance Education.

Smith J.M. (1990) Dance Perspective on the National Curriculum in *Towards the Future: Dance Education in the 1990s*. Dance and the Child International and the National Dance Teachers' Association.

Index